DEBBIE MACOMBER
Love 'n' Marriage

Silhouette Romance

Published by Silhouette Books New York

America's Publisher of Contemporary Romance

SILHOUETTE BOOKS
300 E. 42nd St., New York, N.Y. 10017

Copyright © 1987 by Debbie Macomber

ISBN: 0-373-08522-2

First Silhouette Books printing August 1987

America's Publisher of Contemporary Romance

Printed in the U.S.A.

"Shall we make a wish?"

she asked, feeling happy and excited.

Jonas snorted softly. "Why waste good money?"

"Don't be such a skeptic. It's traditional to throw a coin into a fountain, and what better place than Paris for wishes to come true?"

His eyes revealed exactly what he thought of this exercise. Nonetheless, Jonas reached inside his own pocket and took out a silver dollar.

"That's too much."

"It's a big wish." The silver dollar made a small splash before sinking into the depths.

"Okay, my turn." She closed her eyes and flung a coin over her shoulder. "There."

"Stephanie?" When she didn't respond, Jonas turned, standing directly in front of her. His arms went around her, anchoring her against him. Gently he laid his cheek alongside hers. "Tell me Stephanie," Jonas asked in a hoarse whisper, "did you wish for the same thing I did?"

Their eyes met hungrily and locked. Stephanie nodded, unable to answer. Jonas caught her to him and lowered his mouth to hers.

Dear Reader,

Welcome to Silhouette. Experience the magic of the wonderful world where two people fall in love. Meet heroines who will make you cheer for their happiness, and heroes (be they the boy next door or a handsome, mysterious stranger) who will win your heart. Silhouette Romances reflect the magic of love—sweeping you away with books that will make you laugh and cry, heartwarming, poignant stories that will move you time and time again.

In the next few months, we're publishing romances by many of your all-time favorites, such as Diana Palmer, Brittany Young, Emilie Richards and Arlene James. Your response to these authors and other authors of Silhouette Romances has served as a touchstone for us, and we're pleased to bring you more books with Silhouette's distinctive medley of charm, wit and—above all—*romance*.

I hope you enjoy this book and the many stories to come. Experience the magic!

Sincerely,

Tara Hughes
Senior Editor
Silhouette Books

Books by Debbie Macomber

Silhouette Romance

Silhouette Special Edition

DEBBIE MACOMBER

has quickly become one of Silhouette's most prolific authors. As a wife and mother of four, she not only manages to keep her family happy, but she also keeps her publisher and readers happy with each book she writes.

Chapter One

Stephanie Coulter sauntered into the personnel office at Lockwood Industries carrying a brown paper bag. Her friend, Jan Michaels, glanced up expectantly. "Hi. To what do I owe this unexpected pleasure?"

In response, Stephanie placed the sack on the top of Jan's desk.

"What's that?"

Stephanie sat on the corner of her friend's desk and folded her arms. "Maureen sent the books. It seems I've been allotted the privilege of delivering romances."

"I take it Potter is still sick?"

"Right." The entire morning had been a series of frustrations for Stephanie. Her boss was out with a bad case of the flu for the third consecutive day. For the first couple of days, Stephanie had been able to occupy herself with the little things a secretary never seems to find the time to do. Things like clearing out the filing cabinets and reorganizing her desk. But by the third morning she'd run out of ideas, and had ended up typing a letter to her parents, feeling guilty about doing it on company time.

"Old Stone Face is out as well," Jan informed her.

The uncomplimentary name had been bestowed upon the executive secretary to the company's president, Jonas Lockwood. In the two years that Stephanie had been working for the company, she'd never known Bertha Westheimer to miss a day. For that matter, Stephanie had never even visited the older woman's domain on the top floor, and doubted that she ever would. Bertha guarded her territory like a polar bear protecting her cubs.

The corner of Jan's mouth twitched. "And guess who's working with Mr. Lockwood? You're going to love this."

"Who?" Stephanie mentally reviewed the list of possible candidates, coming up blank.

"Mimi Palmer."

"Who?"

"Mimi Palmer. She's been here about a month, working in the typing pool, and—get this—she's Old Stone Face's niece."

"I can just imagine how that's working out."

"I haven't heard any complaints yet," Jan murmured as she opened the paper bag. "But then it's still early." She took out the top book and shot a questioning glance in Stephanie's direction. "Are you sure you don't want to read one of these? They're great, Steph, and if you're looking to kill time..."

Stephanie held up both palms and shook her head adamantly. "That would look terrific, wouldn't it.

Can you imagine what Potter would say if he walked in and caught me reading one of those?''

"Take one home," Jan offered next.

"No, thanks. I'm just not into romances."

From the look Jan was giving her, Stephanie could tell that her friend wasn't pleased with her response. She knew that several of the other women employees at Lockwood Industries read romances and often traded books back and forth. To be honest, she didn't see why the women found them so enjoyable, but since she hadn't read one she felt she didn't have any right to judge.

"I wish you wouldn't be so closed-minded, especially since—" She was interrupted when the door burst open and Mr. Lockwood himself stormed into the room like an unexpected squall. He was tall and broad-shouldered and walked with a cane, his limp more exaggerated than Stephanie could ever recall seeing it. She remembered the first time she'd seen Jonas Lockwood and the fleeting sadness she'd felt that a man so attractive would be chained so. The twisted right leg marred the perfection of his healthy, strong body. His appearance was that of a cynical, relentless male. As always, Stephanie couldn't take her eyes away from him. His dark good looks commanded her attention anytime he was near.

He paused only a second while his frosty blue gaze ran over her in an emotionless inspection, dismissing her. She wasn't accustomed to anyone regarding her as though she were nothing more than a pesky piece of lint. It infuriated Stephanie even more that his reaction should bother her at all. She hadn't exactly been holding her breath waiting for the company president to notice her. She found him intriguing, and subconsciously had expected some reaction from him once they met. He revealed nothing except irritation.

"Damn it, Michaels, couldn't you find me a decent replacement for even one day?" he roared, completely ignoring Stephanie.

"Mr. Lockwood, sir." Clearing her throat, Jan got to her feet. "Sir, is there a problem?"

"I'd hardly be standing here if there wasn't," he gritted. "Why the hell would you send me that nitwit woman in the first place?"

"Sir, Miss Westheimer recommended Miss Palmer. She told me that Miss Palmer is highly qualified—"

"She's utterly incompetent."

He certainly didn't mince words, Stephanie mused.

"I specifically asked for a mature secretary. Certainly that shouldn't be such a difficult request."

"But, sir..."

"Older, more mature women approach the office with businesslike attitudes, and are far less emotional."

That had to be one of the most unfair cracks Stephanie had ever heard. She bristled involuntarily. "If you'll excuse me for interrupting, I'd like to point out to Mr. Lockwood that a qualified secretary is able to adapt to any given situation. I sincerely doubt that age has anything to do with it."

His sharp eyes blazed over her face. "Who are you?"

"Stephanie Coulter."

"Miss Coulter is Mr. Potter's secretary—"

"Do you always speak out of turn?" He eyed her with open disapproval.

"Only when the occasion calls for it."

"Can you type?"

"One hundred words a minute."

"Shorthand?"

"Yes."

"Follow me."

"But, Mr. Lockwood..." Stephanie felt like a tongue-tied idiot for having spoken out of turn.

"Apparently Ms. Coulter is willing to prove just how qualified she is. She can work for me today. What you tell Potter is no concern of mine." He turned abruptly, obviously expecting Stephanie to trot after him obediently.

Stephanie's gaze clashed with her friend's. "I guess that answers that."

Grinning, Jan pointed in the direction of the elevator. "Good luck."

Stephanie had the distinct feeling she was going to need it.

Walking briskly down the wide corridor, she arrived just as the elevator door parted. She stepped inside, holding herself stiffly.

Jonas Lockwood moved forward and pushed the appropriate button, then stepped back. Stephanie noted that he leaned heavily on the cane. She had trouble remembering the last time she'd seen him use one. More often than not, he walked without it.

The elevator rode silently to the top floor, and the door swished open to reveal a huge open area. His office took up the entire top floor. Half of the area was taken up by an immense reception area with a circular desk in the center.

"This way," he said, giving her a derisive look.

Speechless, Stephanie followed him, awestruck by the plush furniture in the gigantic office. The view of Minneapolis was spectacular, but Stephanie didn't dare stop to appreciate it. Mimi Palmer sat at the large circular desk, sniffling. Her blond hair bounced against the tops of her shoulders as her head bobbed up and down in an effort to curtail her tears. Another man Stephanie didn't recognize was pacing the area near the desk. He glanced up when Jonas and Stephanie approached, and frowned. The man was ruggedly built and of medium height. Stephanie guessed his age to be around forty-five, perhaps a bit older.

"Jonas, I'm sure the young lady didn't mean any harm." The other man spoke for the first time.

Jonas disregarded the man as effectively as he'd ignored Stephanie only moments before. He stepped in front of the crying Mimi and shot a poisonous glance in her direction. "She may have ruined six months of negotiations with her incompetence."

"I'm sorry, s-so sorry," Mimi cried. "I didn't know."

"Not only does she keep an important call on hold for fifteen minutes while she makes a pot of coffee, she insults the company president by asking stupid questions, and then can't locate the file."

Mimi covered her face with her hands and released a high-pitched cry. "I was only trying to help."

Jonas snorted, and Mimi let out another wail.

Stephanie moved forward. "Mimi, stop crying. You're not doing anyone any good. Unless you can help here, I'd suggest you go to the ladies' room and compose yourself." She turned to Jonas. "Tell me the name on the file, and I'll see if I can locate it."

"Phinney."

"I doubt Ms. Palmer lost it. Under pressure, she might have had trouble spelling it." The filing-cabinet drawer shot open as Stephanie located the *Ph*'s and sorted through the neatly organized drawer. Within seconds she located it, pulled it free and handed it to Jonas. "If you'd like, I can phone back and explain. I'll come up with some excuse."

"I'll do it," he barked.

"Fine."

"Now what can I do for you?" She directed her question at the middle-aged man who stood in the center of the room with his mouth hanging open.

"I'm Adam Holmes."

"Mr. Holmes," Stephanie acknowledged briskly. "As I'm sure Mr. Lockwood explained, his secretary is ill for the day, but if I can help you, I'd be most pleased to do so."

He opened his leather briefcase. "I'm here to drop off a few papers for Jonas to read over."

Stephanie took them from his outstretched hand. "I'll see to it that Mr. Lockwood receives these."

"I don't doubt you for an instant," he said with a low chuckle. "Tell Jonas to contact me at my office if he has any questions."

"I'll do that."

The phone beeped, and Stephanie reached for the receiver. "Mr. Lockwood's office," she said in a crisp, professional voice, then wrote down the message, promising the caller that Mr. Lockwood would return the call.

While she was writing down the information, Adam Holmes raised his hand in salute and sauntered toward the elevator. Stephanie watched him go. There was a kindness to his features, and the spark in his dark blue eyes assured her that he was far from old.

The phone rang twice more while Stephanie sorted through the mail. She wrote down the messages and put them in a neat stack, waiting for Jonas to be off the line so she could give them to him.

Mimi reappeared dabbing at the corner of her right eye with a tissue. "I made a mess of things, didn't I?"

"Don't worry about it." Stephanie offered the woman a warm smile with her reassurance. "This job was just more than you were used to handling."

"I'm a good typist."

"I think you must be."

"Aunt Bertha said I wouldn't have any problems for one day."

"Your aunt seems to have underestimated the demands of her position."

"I . . . think she did, too," Mimi said. "Would it be all right if I went back to the typing pool? I don't think I'll be any good around here."

"That'll be fine, Mimi. I'll tell Mr. Lockwood for you."

At the mention of their employer's name, Mimi grimaced. "He's horrible."

Stephanie watched the young blonde leave, furious with Old Stone Face for having put her niece in such an unenviable position. An hour later, however, Stephanie came to agree with Mimi's assessment of her employer. He *was* horrible.

A couple of minutes after Mimi's departure, Jonas called her into his office. Stephanie took the phone messages and the mail with her.

"Take a letter," he said without glancing up from the huge rosewood desk.

Stephanie was too stunned by his cool, unemotional tone to react quickly enough to suit him.

"Do you plan to memorize it?" he said, taunting her.

"Of course not . . ." Stephanie didn't fluster easily, but already this arrogant, unreasonable man had broken through her cool manner. "If you'll excuse me a moment, I'll get a pad and pen."

"That's generally recommended."

No sooner had she reappeared than her employer began dictating his daily correspondence. He barely paused to breathe between letters, obviously expecting her to keep pace with him. When he'd finished, he handed her a pile of financial reports and asked her to type them.

"How soon will you have them ready?" His expressionless blue eyes cut into her. The impatience in his gaze told her that half the day was gone already, and there was business to be done.

"Within the hour," she replied, knowing she'd have to draw upon every skill she'd learned as a secretary to meet her own deadline.

"Good." He lowered his gaze in a gesture of dismissal, and Stephanie returned to the other office, disliking him all the more.

Her fingers fairly flew over the keys, her concentration total. Jonas interrupted her three times to ask for files, but Stephanie was determined to meet her own deadline. She'd have those letters ready or die trying.

Precisely an hour later, smiling smugly, she placed the correspondence on his desk. She stepped back, awaiting his response. Meeting the deadline had demanded that she stretch her abilities to their limits and she anticipated some sort of reaction from her employer.

"Yes?" He raised his head and glared at her.

"Your letters."

"I see that. Are you expecting me to applaud your efforts?"

That was exactly what Stephanie had anticipated. After his derogatory remarks, she felt that her superhuman effort had shot holes in his chauvinistic view of the younger secretary, and she wanted to hear him tell her so.

"Listen, Miss Coulter, I'm paying you a respectable wage. I don't consider it my duty to pat you on the back when you merely do what you've been asked. I have neither the time nor the patience to pander to your fragile ego."

Stephanie felt her face explode with color.

"If you require me to sing your praises every time you complete a task, you can leave right now. I have no use for you. Is that understood?"

"Yes, sir," she managed, furious. This was a rare state for Stephanie, who thought of herself as eventempered and easygoing. Never had she disliked any man more. He was terrible. An ogre. A beast. She pivoted sharply and marched into the reception area, so angry she had to take in deep breaths to control her irritation.

Rolling out her chair, she sat down and took a moment to regain her composure.

She hadn't been back at her desk more than fifteen minutes when the intercom beeped. For one irrational instant she toyed with the idea of ignoring him, then decided against it.

"Yes," she said in her most businesslike tone.

"Take lunch, Miss Coulter. But be back here within the hour. I don't tolerate tardiness."

Stephanie sincerely doubted that this man tolerated much of anything. Everything was done at his convenience and at someone else's expense.

Grabbing her purse, she took the elevator down to the floor where the personnel office was located. Jan was at her desk, and she raised questioning eyes when Stephanie walked in the door.

"Hi, how's it going?"

Slowly shaking her head, Stephanie said, "Fine I think." The lie was only a small one. "Is he always like this?"

"Always." Jan chuckled. "But he doesn't push anyone half as hard as he drives himself."

Stephanie could believe it. "He gave me an hour for lunch, but I think I'm supposed to show my gratitude by returning early."

"I'll join you." Jan used the phone to tell a fellow worker she was taking her lunch hour. Withdrawing her purse from the bottom drawer, she stood.

Although Stephanie hated to admit it, she was full of questions about her surly employer, and she hoped that Jan would supply the answers. For two years, she'd only seen him from a distance, and had been fascinated. From everything she knew about him, which wasn't much, Stephanie wouldn't have believed he could be so surly. Those close to him were intensely loyal, yet she had found him rude and unreasonable.

By the time they arrived, the cafeteria was nearly deserted. Stephanie doubted that many employees took this late a lunch.

They decided to share a turkey sandwich, and each ordered a bowl of vegetable-beef soup. Jan carried the orange plastic tray to a long table.

Stephanie tried to come up with a way of casually introducing the subject of Jonas Lockwood into their conversation without being obvious. She couldn't imagine any secretary, even Bertha Westheimer, lasting more than a week. "Why does he find young secretaries so objectionable?"

"I haven't the slightest idea."

"You know—" Stephanie paused and took a bite of the sandwich "—he'd be handsome if he didn't scowl so much of the time."

Jan answered with a faint nod. "I think Jonas Lockwood must be an unhappy man."

That much was obvious to Stephanie. "Why does he walk with a limp?" He seemed far too young to need a cane. She guessed that he was in his mid-thirties, possibly close to forty. Figuring out his age was difficult, since he'd worn a perpetual frown all morning.

"He had an accident several years ago. Skiing, I think. I once heard the story, but I can't remember the details. Not that he'd ever let anyone know, but I'm sure his leg must ache sometimes. I can tell because he usually goes on a rampage when it hurts. At least that's my theory."

From the short time she'd spent with him, Stephanie guessed that his leg must be killing him. She'd noted the way he'd leaned heavily on the cane in the elevator. Maybe there was a chance that his temperament would improve. But she doubted that it would make any difference to her feelings toward the objectionable man.

Part of the problem, Stephanie realized, was that she was keenly disappointed in him. For two years, she'd been studying Jonas from a distance. Perhaps she'd even romanticized him in the way that Jan and others did with the romances they read. Whatever it was that had fascinated her from afar had been shattered by the reality of what a hot-tempered, unappreciative beast he was.

Jan finished off her soup. "Will you stop in after work?"

"So you can hear the latest horror stories?"

"He's not so bad," Jan claimed. "Really."

"He's the most arrogant, insufferable man I've ever had the displeasure of knowing."

"Give him a day or two to mellow out."

"Never."

Finished with lunch, Stephanie deposited their tray and refilled her coffee cup to take with her to the top floor. When she arrived, the door between the two offices was closed, and she hadn't the faintest idea if Jonas Lockwood was inside or not. Setting the coffee on the desk, she read over the financial reports and cost sheets he'd left on her desk, apparently wanting her to type them. Taking a sip of coffee, she turned the sheet over, her eagle eyes running down the column of figures.

"Welcome back, Miss Coulter." The gruff male voice spoke from behind her. "I see that you're punctual. I approve."

Stephanie bristled. Everyone who worked with Jonas seemed to think he was wonderful. That wasn't the impression Stephanie had. He made her furious, and she struggled to disguise it.

"I would suggest, however, that you stop wasting time and get busy."

"Yes, sir." She tossed him an acid grin. For just an instant, Stephanie thought she caught a flicker of amusement in his electric-blue eyes. But she sincerely doubted that someone as cold as Jonas Lockwood knew how to smile.

As the afternoon progressed, the one word that kept running through Stephanie's mind was *demanding*. Jonas Lockwood didn't ask, he demanded. And when he wanted something, he wanted it that instant, not ten minutes later. He tolerated no excuses and made no allowances for ignorance. If he needed a dossier, she was expected to know what drawer it would be filed in and how to get to it in the most expedient manner. And she was to deliver it to him the instant he asked. If she was a minute late, he didn't hesitate to let her know about his disapproval.

The phone seemed to ring constantly, and when she wasn't answering the phone, she was tending to his long list of demands.

Just when she started typing the financial report, the buzzer rang.

"Yes." If she didn't get the typing done before the end of the day, he would certainly comment. Jonas Lockwood didn't want a mere secretary, he required Wonder Woman. Her low estimation of Bertha Westheimer rose quite a lot.

"Bring me the Johnson file."

"Right away." She moved to the cabinet and groaned as her gaze located three files, all labeled Johnson. Not taking a chance, she pulled all three and set them on his desk. She noted that Jonas was rubbing his thigh, his hand moving up and down his leg in a stroking motion. His brow was marred by thick lines. He seemed to be in such pain that Stephanie paused, not knowing what to say or do.

He glanced up, and the steely look in his eyes grew sharper. "Haven't I given you enough to do, Miss Coulter? Or would you like a few more tasks that need to be completed before you leave tonight?"

Rather than state the obvious, she turned and stepped back to her desk. Sitting at the typewriter, Stephanie couldn't get Jonas out of her mind. There was so much virility in his rugged, dark features, yet for all the emotion he revealed, he could have been cast in bronze. Jonas Lockwood wasn't a man she would be able to forget.

Five o'clock rolled around, and she still had two short reports to finish. It didn't matter how much time it required, Stephanie was determined to stay until every last item he'd given her was completed.

"Hi." Jan stepped off the elevator at five-thirty and greeted her. "I've been waiting for you."

"Sorry." Stephanie rested her hands in her lap. "I've only got a bit more to do."

"Leave it. I'm sure Old Stone Face doesn't expect her desk to be cleared tomorrow morning."

"It isn't what she expects, it's what Mr. Lockwood demands. I've never met anyone like him." She lowered her voice. "Everything is done at his convenience."

"It's his company."

Stephanie shook her head. "Well, listen, I'll trade you bosses any day of the week."

"Is that a fact, Miss Coulter?"

Stephanie managed to swallow a strangled breath. She turned and glared at Jonas, despising him for eavesdropping on a private conversation.

"That'll be all, Miss Coulter. You may leave."

She opened her mouth to argue with him, but decided she'd be a fool to give up the opportunity to escape when it was presented to her. "Thank you. And may I say it was a memorable experience to work for you, Mr. Lockwood."

He'd already turned, refusing to acknowledge her statement.

"However—" she raised her voice, determined that he hear her "—I'd prefer working for a more mature male." She wanted to remind him of his earlier derogatory comments about the fairer sex. "A man over forty is far less demanding, and a thousand times more reasonable and patient."

"Stephanie..." Jan hissed in warning.

"Good day, Miss Coulter." If possible, the icy front he wore like an impenetrable mask froze all the more.

"Goodbye, Mr. Lockwood." With that, she retrieved her purse and marched out of the office, Jan following in her wake.

"Wow, what happened this afternoon?" Jan asked, her eyes sparkling with curiosity.

"Nothing."

"I can tell."

"He wasn't any more objectionable after lunch than he was before. Mr. Jonas Lockwood is simply impossible to work with."

"Well, you two apparently didn't get off on the right foot."

"I'm a fairly patient person. I tried to work with the man. But as far as I'm concerned, there's no excuse for someone to be so outspokenly rude and arrogant. He has no right to take out his ill humor on me or anyone else. There's simply no call for such behavior."

"Right." But one side of Jan's mouth twitched as though she were holding in a laugh.

"You find that amusing?"

"No, not really. I was just thinking that you could be just the woman."

"Just the woman for what?"

"For years the female employees of Lockwood Industries have been waiting for a woman exactly like you, and all the while you were right under our noses."

"What are you talking about?"

"Jonas Lockwood needs a woman with nerves of steel who can stand up to him."

"For what?"

"To bring him down amongst us mortals. We feel that all he needs is to fall in love."

Stephanie couldn't help herself. She snickered. "Impossible. Rocks are incapable of feeling, and that man is about as emotional as marble."

"I'm not so sure," Jan commented. "He works so hard because this business is his life. There's nothing else to fill the emptiness."

"You don't honestly believe a mere woman is capable of changing that?"

"Not just any woman, but someone special."

"Well, leave me out of it."

"You're sure?"

"Absolutely, positively, sure." Although the thought of seeing Jonas Lockwood on his knees was an appealing one, Stephanie was convinced it would never happen. He was too hard. A man like that was incapable of any emotion.

"Oh, I forgot to tell you."

"Tell me what?" From the look on Jan's face, Stephanie could tell she wasn't going to like her friend's next words.

"Bertha Westheimer telephoned this afternoon...."

"And?" Already Stephanie could feel the muscles between her shoulder blades tighten in anticipation.

"And she's apparently recovering."

"Good."

"But, unfortunately, not enough to return to work. It looks like you'll be with Mr. Lockwood another day."

"Oh, no, you don't," Stephanie objected. "I'll quit before I'll work with that beast another minute."

Jan didn't speak for a moment. "In other words, you're willing to let him assume everything he said about younger secretaries is true?"

Chapter Two

"Good morning, Mr. Lockwood." Stephanie looked up from her desk and smiled beguilingly. After a sleepless night, she'd decided to change her tactics. Her mother had always claimed that it was much easier to attract flies with honey. In working with Jonas Lockwood that first day, Stephanie was guilty of giving him a vinegar overdose. Today, she decided, she'd fairly ooze with charm, and drive the poor man crazy. With that thought in mind, she'd dressed for work, humming.

"Morning." Naturally, he didn't reveal any positive reaction to her good-natured greeting.

"There's coffee, if you'd like a cup." She'd arrived an hour early to organize her desk and her day.

"Please." He carried his briefcase into his office.

Stephanie noticed that his limp was barely noticeable this morning. Jan's theory about his leg tying in with his disposition could well be proven within the next ten hours.

Jonas was already seated at his desk by the time Stephanie brought in his coffee. He didn't look up. "I would have thought you'd consider making coffee too menial a task for a woman of your talent."

"Of course not. A good secretary is responsible—"

"I get the picture, Miss Coulter." He cut her off and continued to scan the mail, his concentration centering on the neat stack of letters she'd previously sorted. "I'll need you to take notes during a luncheon meeting, if that would be convenient."

"Of course," she replied sweetly. "Are there any files I should read beforehand to acquaint myself with the subject?"

"Yes." He listed several names and businesses, but for all the notice he gave her, she could well have been a marble statue decorating his office. "One last thing." For the first time he raised his eyes to hers. "Contact personnel and find out how much longer Ms. Westheimer will be out."

It was on the tip of Stephanie's tongue to tell him his precious "mature" secretary couldn't be back soon enough to suit her. "Right away, sir." Her tone dripped honey.

The piercing blue eyes narrowed fractionally. "I think I liked you better when you weren't so subservient. However, I'm pleased that you finally recognize your place."

Stephanie was so furious she wanted to explode. Instead, she smiled until the muscles at the sides of her mouth ached with the effort. "It's only my job, sir."

His eyes sharpened all the more if that was possible. "Exactly, Ms. Coulter."

It took every ounce of self-control Stephanie possessed to disguise her outrage. She'd never had to deal with such a man. But with everything that was in her, she was determined not to cave in to his dislike of her.

They worked together most of the morning, dealing with the mail first. If Jonas spoke to her, it was in the form of clipped requests. They had a job to do, and there was no room for anything else. Not a smile. Not a joke. No unnecessary communication. He seemed to look upon her as a necessary piece of equipment, like the telephone. She was there to see to the smooth running of his business—nothing else. This puzzled Stephanie. She knew she was reasonably good-looking, and yet Jonas treated her with the same emotion he would his briefcase. She was both amused and insulted.

Stephanie had learned earlier that the game was played by Jonas Lockwood's rules. In every other office where she'd been employed, she'd seen herself as part of a team. With Jonas, she was keenly aware that she was only a small spoke in a large wheel. Jonas Lockwood was the wagon.

Once back at her desk, she took a minute to contact Jan before tackling the long list of requests Jonas had given her.

"Jan? Stephanie here. I won't be able to meet you for lunch."

"Do you want me to bring you back something?"

"No, I'm attending a meeting with Mr. Lockwood."

"Hey, that's great. He's never taken Old Stone Face with him before. You must have impressed him."

"I sincerely doubt that. The man is unimpressable."

"Don't be so sure," she said, a smile evident in her voice. "By the way, did you give any thought to what I said yesterday?"

Stephanie could only assume Jan was referring to the challenge of making Jonas Lockwood fall in love. The idea caused her to smother a small laugh. "Yes, I did. You're nuts if you even think I'd attempt anything so crazy."

"He doesn't so much need to be put in his place as to find it. And from what I saw yesterday, you're just the woman to do it."

"Maybe." However, Stephanie sincerely doubted that someone as unemotional as Jonas Lockwood was capable of falling in love. Part of her wanted to rebel at the way he treated her. Rarely had a man been so indifferent toward her. With her even features, smooth ivory skin and soft golden hair, Stephanie was aware that men found her attractive. Jonas Lockwood's blatant indifference was a surprise. When Jonas looked at her, all she felt was a chill that cut straight through her bones.

"Steph? Are you there?"

"Oh, sorry, I was just thinking."

"I hope that means what I think it means. Listen, I'd like to get together with you soon. There's something we—I—want to talk over with you."

"If it has to do with you-know-who, forget it!"

Chuckling, Jan said, "I'll see you later."

"Right."

Replacing the telephone receiver, Stephanie wheeled her chair to the typewriter and inserted a piece of paper. She worked with only a few interruptions for the next two hours. A half hour before the scheduled luncheon, she sorted through the list of files Jonas had recommended in order to familiarize herself with the people she'd be meeting.

She felt mentally prepared and alert for the coming luncheon. When Jonas appeared, she stood wordlessly and followed him into the elevator. Knowing that he was a man who didn't appreciate unnecessary conversation, Stephanie kept her comments and questions to herself. She would have her answers eventually.

A driver was waiting outside the building, and he held open the car door for Jonas and Stephanie as they approached.

Stephanie climbed inside, her fingers absently investigating the smooth velvet interior of the limo. Almost immediately, Jonas opened his briefcase and took out a file.

She eyed him curiously. She might have a low opinion of him as a human being, but his knowledge and business acumen were beyond question. He was a man born to lead. Just from working with him these two days, Stephanie had witnessed his swift, decisive nature. When he saw something, he went after it by the most direct route. Life had no gray areas for a man of his nature—it was either black or white, with no middle ground.

She found her gaze wandering to his hands. They were large, with blunt nails and short wisps of dark hair curled out from the French cuffs of his shirt. His hands looked capable of forging an empire or tenderly caressing a woman. He could be gentle—his hands told her as much. The thought of his large hands stroking her smooth skin did funny things to her breathing. The ridiculousness of such a notion caused Stephanie to shake her head. A funny sound slid from the back of her throat, and Jonas glanced up momentarily.

Quickly, Stephanie looked out the side window, wondering what was happening to her. She didn't even like this man.

As the limo pulled up to a huge skyscraper, Jonas announced, "I want you to take notes on the meeting. When we return, type them up and give me your impressions of what happened."

Stephanie opened and closed her mouth in surprise. She was his secretary, not his personal analyst. But she knew better than to question the mighty Jonas Lockwood. She'd do as he asked and accomplish it with a smile. He'd have no reason to find fault with her.

They rode the elevator to the twenty-first floor of the Bellerman Building. The heavy doors slid open, and Jonas directed her into the meeting room at the end of the narrow hallway. Ten chrome chairs upholstered in moss green were strategically placed around a long rosewood table. Jonas claimed the seat at the end and motioned for Stephanie to take the chair at his side. She was faintly surprised that he wanted her so close at hand. Since she was a mere woman, and a young one at that, Stephanie had expected to sit in a corner and observe the proceedings from there.

Lunch was served, and what followed was a lesson in business that she hadn't learned in her four years as an executive secretary. There was a layered feel to the meeting. She took meticulous notes of the statements that were made, but Stephanie wondered at the underlying meaning of the words. She was impressed by the role Jonas played. He appeared to be in complete charge of the subjects discussed without speaking himself, determining the course of the meeting with a nod of his head or a small movement of his hand. At first glance, anyone looking in would assume that Jonas was bored by the entire proceedings. The man was unnerving.

At precisely two, it was over. Stephanie looked up from her steno pad and flexed her tired shoulder muscles. As the other men stood, the sounds of brief-cases opening and closing filled the spacious room.

"Good to see you again, Lockwood." The man sitting on Jonas's right made the comment, and his gaze slid over Stephanie with a familiarity that left a bad taste in her mouth. "Leave it to you to have the most beautiful woman in Minneapolis as your private secretary."

Jonas's cutting blue gaze left the man to rest momentarily on Stephanie. "She's a substitute. My secretary is ill this week." He didn't give her a moment more of his attention as he stood and reached for his cane, leaving her to follow him.

Fuming that he would treat her so dismissively, Stephanie reached for her purse. He hadn't noticed anything about her but her secretarial skills. She was a woman, and if Jonas Lockwood didn't recognize that, it was his problem, not hers. Yet she was offended by his comment, and she stewed about it all the way back to Lockwood Industries.

The phone rang ten minutes after Stephanie was seated at her desk. "Mr. Lockwood's office."

"Steph, it's Jan. I talked with Bertha Westheimer this afternoon, and I have good news."

"I could do with some," she grumbled.

"She'll be back Monday morning."

"And not a minute too soon."

"How'd the luncheon meeting go?"

"I...I don't know." She hadn't sorted through her notes enough to analyze what had transpired. "It was interesting."

"See, he's already having an affect on you."

"He?" she said, teasing Jan. "I can't possibly believe you mean who I think."

Jan's answer was a smothered giggle. "Don't forget to meet me at five-thirty. On second thought, I'll come up for you."

"Fine. And thanks for the *good* news. I could do with a lot more."

The remainder of the afternoon was surprisingly peaceful. Stephanie typed up her notes and observations and placed them on Jonas's desk before she left.

He was writing something; he paused and glanced up. "Yes?"

"I just wanted to tell you that Ms. Westheimer will be back Monday morning. It's been an education working with you for the past couple of days."

He leaned back in his chair and looked at her steadily. "Not a pleasure? You filled in nicely. Quite a surprise, Miss Coulter."

Stephanie supposed that this was as much of a compliment as she could expect from such a man. "Now that's something I'm pleased to hear," she said, smiling despite the effort not to.

"I'm convinced you'll do well at Lockwood Industries."

"Thank you. And if ever you need a replacement for Ms. Westheimer..."

"I'm hoping that won't be soon."

Not as much as I am, Stephanie mused. "Good day, Mr. Lockwood."

He'd already returned to his work. "Good evening, Miss Coulter."

Stephanie's heart was pounding by the time she met Jan Michaels. For an instant there, she could almost have liked Jonas Lockwood. Almost, but not quite.

"I take it the afternoon ran smoothly."

"Relatively so," Stephanie confirmed.

"Are you ready to talk?"

"It depends on the subject. Jonas Lockwood is off-limits."

"Unfair," Jan objected. "You know I want to discuss our infamous boss. Come on, I'll buy you a drink and loosen your tongue."

"That's what I'm worried about."

"Stop complaining. Don't check the olive in a gift drink."

"What?" Stephanie asked, laughing.

"Oh nothing, I was just trying to make a joke. You know the old saying about not checking the teeth in a gift horse? It's Friday, and it's been a long week." Folding her jacket over her arm, Jan led the way down the elevator and through the wide glass doors of the Lockwood Industries building. The Sherman Street traffic was snarled in the evening rush hour, and Jan wove her way between the stalled cars to a small cocktail lounge a couple of blocks from the building.

A small table of women waved when they entered the lounge. Stephanie recognized several faces.

"Hi, everyone. You all know Stephanie." Jan placed her arm over Stephanie's shoulder.

"Hi." Stephanie raised her hand in greeting.

"Meet Barbara and Toni." Jan continued the introductions with, "You know Maureen."

"Well, what do you think, ladies?"

"She's great."

"Perfect."

"Exactly what we want."

Taking a chair, Stephanie glanced around the small group, shaking her head in wonder. "What are you guys talking about?"

"You!" All four spoke at once.

"Does this have to do with Jonas Lockwood?" Already she didn't like the sound of this.

"You didn't tell her?" The brunette, Toni, questioned Jan.

"I think we'd better order her a drink first."

Still shaking her head with wonder, Stephanie glanced from one expectant face to the other. The four women came in various forms and ages. Barbara had to be over forty, Toni in her mid-thirties, Maureen younger, and Jan, who Stephanie guessed was near her own age of twenty-four.

The cocktail waitress returned with five bottles of sparkling wine cooler.

"Now, what's this all about?" Stephanie questioned, growing more curious by the minute.

"I think we should start at the beginning," Jan suggested.

"Please," Stephanie murmured.

"You see, we all read romances. We're hooked on them. They're wonderful stories."

"Right. And Jonas Lockwood makes *the* perfect hero, don't you think?" Barbara added.

"Pardon?" To Stephanie's way of thinking, he made *the* perfect block of ice.

"Haven't you noticed that chiseled leanness he has about him?"

"And those craggy male features?"

"I suppose," Stephanie muttered, growing more confused by the minute. To ease some of the dryness in her throat, she took a long swallow of the wine cooler. It was surprisingly refreshing.

"He's got that cute little cleft in his chin."

Now that was something Stephanie hadn't noticed.

"The four of us have decided that Mr. Lockwood is really an unhappy man," the redhead, Maureen, continued. "His life is empty."

"He needs a woman to love, and one who will love him," Barbara said.

"That's an interesting theory," Stephanie said, reaching for the wine a second time. She had to watch how much she consumed, or the four of them would soon be making sense.

"It's obvious that one of us won't be his true love," Toni added.

"What about you, Jan?" Stephanie pointed her drink in her friend's direction.

"Sorry, but I'm seriously contemplating marriage."

"Only Jim doesn't know it yet," Maureen piped in. Everyone laughed.

"But what has all this got to do with me?"

"You're perfect for Jonas Lockwood—just the type of woman he needs."

"Just the heroine type. Attractive and bright."

"Spunky," Jan tossed in.

"I can't believe what I'm hearing," Stephanie protested. "I don't even like the man."

"That's all the better. The heroines in the romances seldom do, either."

"I think you ladies are confusing fantasy with reality."

"Of course we are. That's the fun of it. We're all incurable romantics, and when we see a romance in the making it's simply part of our nature to want to step in and help things along."

"We've even thought about writing one," Toni informed her.

"But why me?"

"You're perfect for Mr. Lockwood, in addition to being exceptionally attractive."

"Thanks, but . . ."

"And you don't seem to lord it over those of us who aren't," Barbara murmured.

"But that doesn't explain why you chose me to weave your plot around."

"Mr. Lockwood likes you."

"Oh, hardly—"

"All right, he respects you. We all noticed that this afternoon when you left for the meeting. He wouldn't take you along if he didn't value your opinion."

Choking on a mouthful of wine, Stephanie shook her head wildly. "Do you know what he said? A man commented on what an attractive secretary he had, and your hero Lockwood told him I was a substitute, as though he'd had to scrape the bottom of the barrel to come up with me." Finding the situation unbelievably hysterical now, Stephanie giggled. It took her a moment to notice that the other four were strangely quiet.

"What do you think, Maureen?" Jan looked at the redhead.

"I'd stay he has definitely noticed her. He's fighting it already."

"Ladies, ladies, you've got this blown out of all proportion."

"I don't think so." Jan reached for her purse, and withdrew a copy of Stephanie's employment application. "I did a bit of checking here. You had two employers in the two years before you came to us. Right?"

"Right." Stephanie's hand folded around her wineglass as she shifted uncomfortably.

"Why?"

"Well." She paused to clear her throat. "I've had some problems with the men I've worked with."

"What kind of problems?"

"You know." She waved her hand.

"Men making advances?" Toni, the quiet one, suggested.

"More than that. They all seemed to require more than secretarial duties of me, if you get my meaning."

"We do," Jan said.

"Trust me, ladies, it wasn't romance my former bosses had in mind." Just thinking of those stress-filled days produced an involuntary grimace.

"What did you do?"

"The only thing I could. I quit."

"Yes, she's heroine material all right," Toni said with a curt nod.

Unable to hold back a laugh, Stephanie added, "You ladies don't honestly believe all this, do you?"

"You bet we do," all four concurred.

"But why would it matter to you if Jonas Lockwood is married or not? Maybe he's utterly content being single. Marriage isn't for everyone."

Jan answered first. "As I explained, we're all incurable romantics. We've worked for Mr. Lockwood a lot longer than you. He needs a wife, only he doesn't realize it. But we're doing this for selfish reasons, too. It would help the situation at work for us all if Mr. Lockwood had a family of his own."

"Family?" Stephanie nearly choked on her wine. "First you have me falling in love with him, then we get married, and now I'm bearing his children." This conversation was going from the sublime to the ridiculous. To be honest, she was half-tempted to practice her feminine wiles on Jonas Lockwood, just for the pleasure of seeing if the mighty man would crumble at her feet. Then she would have the ultimate pleasure of snubbing him and walking away. But this clearly wasn't what Jan and friends had in mind.

"You see," Barbara inserted, "we feel that Mr. Lockwood would be more agreeable to certain employee benefits if he walked in our shoes for a while."

Dumbfounded, Stephanie shook her head. These ladies were actually serious. "I think a union would be the more appropriate way to deal with this."

"There isn't one. So we're creating our own—of sorts."

Stephanie still didn't understand. "What kind of benefits?"

"More lenient rules regarding maternity leave."

"Extra days off at Christmas."

"Increased health benefits to include family members."

Lifting the blond curls off her forehead, Stephanie looked around the table at the four intense faces studying her. "You're really serious, aren't you?"

"Completely."

"Utterly."

"We mean business."

"Indeed." Jan raised her hand and called for the waitress, ordering another round.

"I'm really sorry, ladies, but I'm not heroine material." The waitress delivered another round of wine coolers and Stephanie waited until the woman had finished. "A man like Jonas Lockwood needs a woman far less opinionated than me. In two days, we barely said a civil word to each other."

"The woman who loves him will need a strong personality."

"She'd need more than that." Stephanie couldn't imagine any woman capable of tearing down Jonas Lockwood's icy facade. He was too hard, too cold, too unapproachable.

"Say, I didn't know you spoke French." Jan glanced up from Stephanie's application, her eyes growing larger by the minute. "Do you, Steph?"

"My grandmother was French. She insisted I learn."

"Then you're bilingual?"

"Right."

All four women paused, regarding Stephanie as though she had suddenly turned into an alien from outer space. "Hey, why are you looking at me like that?"

"No reason." Barbara lowered her head, apparently finding the maraschino cherry floating in her drink overwhelmingly interesting.

"So your grandmother was French?" Toni asked, doing her best to hide a smile.

"Why do I have the feeling that you four have something dangerously powerful up your sleeves?" Stephanie glanced from one grinning face to the other.

"What does the fact that I speak French fluently have to do with anything?"

"You'll see."

"I don't like the sounds of this," Stephanie muttered.

"What do you think of our idea?" Barbara asked bravely.

"You mean about finding a woman for Mr. Lockwood?"

The four nodded, watching her expectantly.

"Great. As long as that woman isn't me."

"I think it's fate," Jan added. "This couldn't be turning out any better than if we'd planned it."

"Planned what?"

"You'll see," all four echoed.

Monday morning, Stephanie arrived for work early. She'd spent a peaceful weekend, planting a small herb garden in narrow redwood planters and placing them on her patio. Living in a small apartment didn't leave much room for her to practice her gardening skills. The year before, she'd rented a garden space through the parks department. This year, she'd decided to try her green thumb on herbs.

Jan was at her desk when Stephanie arrived at coffee-break time. As much as possible, Stephanie had tried to blot out Friday evening's conversation with Jan and her friends. It appeared that the four had some hideous plot in mind. But she'd quickly squelched that. Even imagining Jonas Lockwood in love was enough to amuse her. It'd never happen. The man had no emotions. That wasn't blood that ran through his veins—it was ink from profit-and-loss statements. He wasn't like ordinary humans.

"Oh, I'm glad you're here," Jan murmured.

"You are?" Already Stephanie was leery. "Ms. Westheimer's fully recovered, hasn't she?"

"Yes, she's here. At least, I assume she is. I haven't heard any rumblings from above."

Stephanie felt a sense of relief. The less she saw of Jonas Lockwood, the better.

"I've made arrangements with your boss for you to be gone next week."

"Arrangements?" Stephanie repeated surprised. "What are you talking about?"

"Do you want to get together at lunch?" Jan asked, ignoring Stephanie's question.

"Jan, what's going on?"

"You'll see."

"Jan!"

"I'll talk to you later." She glanced at her watch. "I'd tell you, honest, but I can't . . . yet."

Disgruntled, Stephanie returned to her office, pausing on the way to question Maureen, who gave her a look of pure innocence. Stephanie didn't know what the two had up their sleeves, but she knew it involved Jonas Lockwood.

The remainder of the morning ran so smoothly that Stephanie was surprised to note that it was lunchtime. She was convinced that working for anyone other than Jonas Lockwood would be a breeze. Mr. Potter, her grandfatherly boss, was patient and undemanding, a pleasant change from the man who barked orders at her as though she were a robot. And Mr. Potter was free with his praise and approval of her efforts. Getting a compliment from Jonas Lockwood was like pulling teeth.

Her lunch was spent with Jan, Maureen and the two others she'd met Friday evening, so there wasn't an opportunity to corner Jan and ask her to explain her comment about finding a replacement for her the following week.

The ladies were all a fun-loving group, quick-witted and personable. Stephanie was relieved when no mention of their infamous employer entered the conversation; in fact, she was more than grateful. Despite all her claims to the contrary, Stephanie had been thinking a lot about Jonas.

On her way back to her office, Stephanie happened to run into the big boss himself. She was waiting for the elevator, checking her makeup with a small hand mirror. The elevator came to a halt, and its wide doors opened. Stephanie came eye-to-eye with her former boss.

"Good day, Miss Coulter."

Stephanie didn't lower the tube of lipstick, her mouth gaping open as she prepared to glide the color across her bottom lip. She was too stunned to move.

"Are you or are you not taking the elevator?"

"Oh, yes," she mumbled, hurrying in next to him. She quickly stuck her mirror and lipstick inside her purse, pressing her lips together to even out the pale summer-rose color.

Jonas placed both hands on his cane. "And how are you doing, Miss Coulter?"

"Exceptionally well. Everyone I've worked with *lately* has appreciated my efforts."

"Perhaps your skills have improved."

If it hadn't been such a drastic idea, Stephanie would have kicked the cane out of his hand. The man was unbearable. "As you suggest," she said with a false sweetness in her voice, "things have definitely improved."

His mouth quirked upwards in something resembling a smile. "I admit to missing your quick wit. Perhaps we'll have the opportunity to exchange insults again sometime soon."

A joke from Jonas Lockwood—all right, an almost joke. Stephanie couldn't believe it.

"Don't count on it." The elevator came to a grinding halt, and the door swooshed open. "Perhaps in another lifetime, Mr. Lockwood."

"You disappoint me, Miss Coulter. I'd looked forward to next week." The doors glided shut.

Next week. Once again those words had been tossed in her direction. She'd let Jan get away without telling her at lunch, but she wasn't waiting another minute. She hurried down the hall to Jan's office.

"All right, explain yourself," she demanded, placing both hands on the edge of her friend's desk.

"About what?" Jan was the picture of innocence, which was a sure sign the woman was up to something.

"I just saw Mr. Lockwood, and he said something about next week. I don't like the sound of this."

"Oh, I guess I forgot to tell you, didn't I?"

"Tell me what?" Stephanie straightened; a strange sensation, akin to dread, shot up and down her spine.

"Mr. Lockwood's traveling to Paris on business."

Crossing her arms, Stephanie glared at Jan suspiciously. "That's nice."

"The interesting part is that he requires a bilingual secretary to accompany him."

Knowing what was coming, Stephanie tightened her jaw until her teeth ached. "You couldn't possibly mean..."

"When Mr. Lockwood first approached personnel, we didn't have anyone on file who spoke French, but since that time I've gone through the applications and found yours."

"Jan, I refuse to go. The man and I don't get along."

"When I mentioned you to Mr. Lockwood, he was delighted."

"I'll just bet."

"Your flight leaves early Monday morning."

Chapter Three

The jet tilted its wings to the right, aligning its narrow bulk with the smooth runway before beginning its descent. Stephanie stared out the small window, fascinated by the breathtaking view of the River Seine far below. Her heart pounded with excitement. Paris. How her grandmother would have envied her. As a young French war bride, Stephanie's grandmother had often longed to revisit the charming French city. Now Stephanie would see it for her.

"If you would tear your gaze from the window a minute, Miss Coulter, we could get some work done," Jonas Lockwood stated sarcastically.

"Of course." Instantly she was all business, reaching for her steno pad. This was the only level on which she could communicate with Jonas. Not once since they'd taken off from Minneapolis-St. Paul International Airport had her employer taken note of the spectacular scenery. No doubt he would have considered it a waste of valuable time.

"I've ordered us a three-bedroom suite at the Château Frontenac," he informed her coolly.

Stephanie silently repeated the name of the hotel. "It sounds lovely."

Jonas glanced down at the paper in his lap and shrugged one muscular shoulder. "I suppose."

It was all Stephanie could do not to shout at him to open his eyes and look at the beauty of the world that surrounded him. At times like these, she wanted to shake Jonas. The mere thought of even touching the stone man produced an involuntary smile. He'd hate being touched.

The middle-aged man Stephanie had met that first morning, Adam Holmes, had accompanied them. He'd been properly introduced, but the role he was to perform in the transaction was left to conjecture. Stephanie guessed that Adam was an attorney.

"It's looks like we're in for pleasant weather," Adam stated conversationally. His dark eyes narrowed fractionally as he gazed out the small window. For most of the trip, Adam had carried the conversation. He was both friendly and outgoing, a blatant contrast to the solemn, serious Jonas.

A little surprised, Stephanie glanced up, not knowing if Adam was addressing his comment to her. Jonas didn't respond. Stephanie would have been shocked to learn that any type of weather interested her employer.

"I would guess early summer is the perfect time to visit Paris." In reality, Stephanie wondered how much of the city she'd have a chance to see. Her one hope was that she would visit the Champs de Mars and view the 934¼-foot Eiffel Tower built for the 1889 World's Fair. High on her list were the twelfth-century cathedral of Notre Dame, and the Arc de Triomphe. She'd spent a year in France as an exchange student in high school, but apart from a quick trip through the airport, Stephanie hadn't seen anything of Paris.

The plane began its descent, and she clicked her seat belt into place. Casually, Jonas put away his papers and closed his briefcase. As soon as they landed they'd be going through customs, and Stephanie would be expected to step into her role as translator. Although she spoke fluent French, it'd been a while since she'd had the opportunity to use it.

To her surprise, everything went without a hitch at the customs station, and her confidence grew. The three moved from that area to the waiting limo with only the minimum of delay.

Adam Holmes held the door open for Stephanie, and she climbed inside the luxurious automobile. Jonas followed her, and they were soon on their way.

At the hotel, they were escorted to their rooms and their luggage was delivered promptly. While Stephanie unpacked her clothes, she heard Jonas and Adam discussing the project. Apparently they would be meeting a powerful financier in the hope of obtaining financial backing for a current project. Lockwood Industries was the world's largest manufacturer of small-airplane parts. There also seemed to be the possibility of establishing a branch of the Minneapolis firm in France, and Jonas had decided on Paris as the first foreign site of Lockwood Industries.

"Miss Coulter."

"Yes." Responding instantly to the command in Jonas's voice, Stephanie appeared in the doorway of her room.

"Lunch will be served in ten minutes."

"I'll be ready. I just need a few minutes to freshen up."

"Of course."

Stephanie doubted that he'd even heard her speak. He'd often given her that impression. Returning to her assigned room, she glanced in the mirror. Several tendrils of soft blond hair had escaped from the coil at the base of her neck. Rather than tuck them back, Stephanie pulled out the pins and reached for her brush. The blond length curled under naturally at her shoulders. When working in the office, she preferred to keep her hair up. It gave her a businesslike look and feel, and that was important around Jonas.

"Miss Coulter."

Taking her brush with her, Stephanie moved into the large central room where Jonas and Adam were waiting.

"Yes?"

For a moment, the room went still as Jonas caught her gaze. Their eyes met and locked. His deep blue eyes narrowed, and an expression of surprise and bewilderment flickered across his lean face. Something showed in his eyes that she couldn't define—certainly not admiration, perhaps astonishment, even shock. His mouth parted slightly as if he wanted to speak, then instantly returned to a stern line.

Adam Holmes's face broke into a spontaneous smile as his lingering gaze swept her appreciatively from head to toe. "I don't think I realized how attractive your secretary is, Jonas."

The muscles in Jonas's jaw looked as though they were cramped. He ran an impatient hand through his hair and turned to reach for his briefcase.

"You wanted me?" It was hard to believe that breathless voice was hers. She sounded as though she'd been running a marathon. She couldn't be attracted to Jonas. He was the last person in the world she wanted to have any romantic feelings for. Normally she was a levelheaded person, not the sort who let her emotions carry her away. Not that Jonas Lockwood was worthy of a moment's consideration. He was arrogant and...

"We'll meet you downstairs." He interrupted her thoughts, his voice cool and unemotional.

"I'll be there in a minute."

"Take your time," he said, doing his best to avoid her.

She turned to go back into her room, but not before she caught the darting look Adam Holmes gave them both, disbelief etched clearly on his smooth, handsome features.

After closing the door, Stephanie sank onto the end of the bed. There must be some virus in the air for her to be thinking this way about Jonas Lockwood. For a moment, she'd actually found him overwhelmingly, unabashedly appealing. She'd actually been physically attracted to him. She shook her head at the wonder of it. She was playing right into Jan's and the other gals' hands. Jonas had noticed her as well—really noticed her. At least his comment when Adam complimented her wasn't that "she was only a substitute." A small smile tugged at the edge of her mouth. Maybe, just maybe, Jonas Lockwood didn't have a heart of ice after all. Perhaps under that glacial front there was a warm, loving man. The thought was so incongruous with the mental picture she held of him that Stephanie shook her head to dispel the image. Without wasting further time inventing nonsensical fantasies about her employer, Stephanie finished styling her hair and changed clothes.

Lunch passed without incident, as did the first series of meetings.

In bed that evening, Stephanie's thoughts spun. They'd called it an early night, but she wasn't able to sleep. The most beautiful city in the world lay at her doorstep, and she would be tied up in meetings for the entire visit. Sitting up, she wiped a hand across her face. She was undecided. They would only be in Paris another two nights. If this was to be her only opportunity, she'd take it now.

Dressing silently, she slipped the hotel key into her purse and carefully tiptoed across the carpet, letting herself out.

Since their hotel was in an older section of the city, she caught a taxi and instructed the friendly driver to take her to several points of interest. He escorted her through Les Halles, the mammoth central food market, which had once been located on the north of the river, but had been moved to Rungis, in the suburbs of Paris.

From there, the talkative cabby drove her past Notre Dame cathedral, pointing out the sights as he went. But Stephanie barely heard him. Her thoughts were focused on that moment in the hotel room earlier in the afternoon when Jonas had looked at her for perhaps the first time. Her hands grew clammy just thinking about it. At the time, she'd been flippant. Now she was profoundly affected. Just remembering it caused her pulse to react. In those brief seconds,

Jonas had seen her as a woman and, just as importantly, she'd viewed him as a man. She was intensely attracted to him and had been for weeks, she just wouldn't admit it.

The driver, chatting easily in French, pointed out the sights, but instead of seeing the magnificent beauty in the buildings that surrounded her, Stephanie's thoughts revolved around Jonas. She wondered about him as a child, and what pain there'd been in his youth to snuff out the joy in his life.

Straightening, she shook her head and asked him in French, "Please take me back to the hotel."

The driver gave her a funny look. *"Oui."*

Stephanie had hoped to see the Louvre, but it wouldn't have been open at this time of night. As it was, she didn't seem to be able to view any of the sights without including Jonas in what she saw. It was useless to pretend otherwise.

Back at the hotel, she gave the driver a generous tip and thanked him. The lobby was quiet, and the soft strains of someone playing the piano sounded in the distance. Stephanie briefly toyed with the idea of stopping in the lounge for a nightcap, but quickly rejected the idea. She wouldn't have any problems sleeping now.

Being extra-cautious not to make any unnecessary noise, Stephanie silently slipped inside the hotel room. She was halfway across the floor when the harsh voice ripped into her.

"Miss Coulter, I didn't bring you to Paris to sneak out in the middle of the night."

Stephanie reacted with a startled gasp, her hand flying to her breast.

"Just who were you meeting? Some young lover?" The words were spoken with a sharp cutting edge, mocking and bitter.

"No. Of course not." She could barely make out Jonas's form in the shadows. He sat facing her, but his features were hidden by the dark.

"Surely you don't expect me to believe that. I understand you spent a year in France. Surely you met some young men."

The words to tell him what to do with his nasty suspicions burned on the tip of her tongue. Instead, she shook her head and replied softly, "I don't know anyone in Paris. I couldn't sleep. It may sound foolish, but I decided that I might not get the opportunity to see the sights, so I—"

"You don't honestly expect me to believe you were out sight-seeing?" The shadow began to move, and Stephanie noted that his hand was massaging his thigh.

Against her will, her heart constricted at the agony she knew his leg was causing him. With everything that was in her, she yearned to ease that pain. She took a tentative step in his direction, claiming the chair across from him. In low, soft tones, she told him about the historic buildings she'd visited and the chatty taxicab driver who had given her a private tour of the older sections of Paris, along with a colorful account of his own ancestry.

Her eyes adjusted to the dark, and she watched as the cynical quirk of his mouth gradually relaxed. "It's really an exceptionally lovely city," she ended by saying.

"Holmes is attracted to you."

"Adam Holmes?" Stephanie couldn't believe what she was hearing, and quickly dismissed the suggestion. "I'm sure you're mistaken."

"Do you find it so surprising?"

"Yes... n-no."

"It's only natural that he find you lovely. As you said, you're in one of the most beautiful cities in the world. It's springtime. You're single, Holmes is single. What's there to discourage a little romance?"

"I hardly know the man."

"Does it matter?"

"Of course it does." Stephanie sighed. She dropped her gaze, sorry now that she'd made the effort to turn aside angry words and be friendly. The man was impossible.

"You could do worse. Adam Holmes is a bright attorney with a secure future."

"If I were buying stock in the man, I might be interested. But we're talking about two people here. I find Adam Holmes friendly and knowledgeable, but I have no romantic interest in him. I'm simply not attracted to him."

"Who does attract you?"

Stephanie swallowed uncomfortably as she battled back the instinctive response. Jonas attracted her. She was still shocked by the realization, but she wasn't willing to hand him that weapon. "I believe my private life is none of your affair," she informed him crisply.

"So there is someone." Impatience surged through his clipped response.

"I didn't say that." Bounding to her feet, she stalked over to the window and hugged her waist. "There's no use even trying to talk to you, is there?"

Her voice revealed her distress. "We seem incapable of maintaining even a polite conversation."

"Does that disappoint you?"

Stephanie could feel his gaze run over her; it seemed to caress her with its intensity—and to demand an answer.

"Yes," she admitted gently. "Very much. There's so much locked up inside you that I don't understand."

"I'm not a puzzle waiting to be solved."

"In some ways you are."

Jonas rubbed a hand over his face. "I can't see that this conversation will get us anywhere."

Stephanie couldn't either. She was tired, Jonas was unreasonable and in pain. The best thing she could do now was to leave the conversation for a more appropriate time. "Good night, Jonas." She didn't wait for his acknowledgement before she headed for her room.

"Good night, Stephanie."

It wasn't until she had changed into her cotton pajamas that Stephanie realized that for the first time since meeting Jonas Lockwood, he'd used her first name. No longer was she a robot who responded to his clipped demands. Somehow, in some way, she had become a woman with flesh and blood. The realization was enough to send her spirits soaring. Hugging the extra pillow beside her, Stephanie held it to her breast and drifted into a sound sleep, content with her world.

"Good morning," Adam greeted her early the following morning. From the looks of the table, Jonas and Adam had been at it for hours.

"Morning." Stephanie walked across the room and poured steaming coffee into the dainty cup, then held it to her mouth with both hands.

"I trust you slept well, Miss Coulter," Jonas inserted next.

So they were back to that. "Thank you, *Mr. Lockwood*, I slept very well."

Jonas glanced up momentarily, and Stephanie recognized the glint of amusement in his eyes. A brief smile moved across his mouth.

"Would you like a croissant?" Adam asked, preparing to lift the flaky pastry onto a china plate with a pair of metal tongs.

"No, thanks." Actually, she might have liked one, but feared a simple thing like accepting a breakfast roll would encourage Adam. She hadn't noticed it the day before, but the eagerness glinting in his gaze revealed the truth of Jonas's statement. Adam Holmes was interested in her. After she was done with her coffee, she'd eat something.

As it turned out, Stephanie barely had time to down the coffee before Jonas stood. "We have a lot of ground to cover today."

He limped to the door without his cane. Stephanie noticed that he preferred not to use it, and did so only when absolutely necessary. His leg had kept him up last night and would soon be aching again without the cane.

"In that case," she said, "you'll want your cane."

Jonas expelled his breath. "Miss Coulter, I require a secretary-translator, not a mother."

"Your leg was bothering you yesterday." She knew she was on dangerously thin ice. Not once had she mentioned his limp. "I see no reason to aggravate it further."

He didn't answer her, but Stephanie noted triumphantly that he reached for his cane before they left the suite.

What followed was a day Stephanie was not likely to forget. The first meeting that morning was a marathon exchange of proposals and counterproposals. They adjourned briefly for lunch, and were at it again before she had the opportunity to take more than a bite or two of her salad.

The afternoon was just as bizarre. No sooner had she finished translating one statement than Jonas gave her another. He was tense, although he didn't show it. Much of the conversation went completely over her head, but in the weeks since meeting Jonas, Stephanie had gained valuable insight into her employer. For the meeting, he almost seemed to wear a bronze mask that revealed none of his feelings or emotions. This was business, just as most of his life was business, with little room for fun and games. If Stephanie had accepted what she saw on the surface, Jonas would have frozen her out completely. But she'd seen a rare glimpse of the man inside, and she'd been intrigued.

The afternoon session was both complicated and challenging. Stephanie noted that Jonas was cool to the point of being aloof, as though what they were discussing was of little consequence to him. Like a gambler, he placed his money on the line for the pleasure of tossing the dice. He enjoyed the thrill, the excitement, and had poured his whole life into it.

During the long afternoon session, Adam Holmes drifted in and out of the room, returning with one document and then another.

It was early evening when the meeting came to an end. Jonas and his French counterpart stood and shook hands.

"We're breaking until morning," Jonas informed Adam outside the conference-room door. "Did you locate that paper on the export tax I asked about earlier?"

"I have them with me," Adam responded, tapping the side of his briefcase.

"I'll want to look them over tonight."

For her part, Stephanie was exhausted and hungry. After no breakfast, she'd barely had time to touch her lunch and her stomach protested strenuously.

Once they were back in the hotel suite, Stephanie immediately slipped off her shoes. They were new, and pinched her heel. Sitting on the sofa, she crossed her legs and rubbed the tender portion of her foot, suspecting a blister.

On the other side of the room Jonas was drilling Adam about one thing or another. She couldn't have cared less. But she had noticed that his gaze rested on her slender legs. When he realized she'd caught the direction of his glance, he turned his head. He looked tired, worn down. She wanted to suggest that he take this evening to rest, but after her comment that morning about his cane, she realized she'd be pressing her luck. She was too weary to fight with Jonas now.

"I'll get that statement for you as quickly as possible," Adam said, rising to his feet.

"Thanks."

The room seemed oddly quiet after Adam left.

"Miss Coulter, order a car."

Stephanie couldn't believe it. The man was a slave driver. Reaching for the phone, she contacted the desk and asked that they have a car available. "How soon do you want it?" she asked, holding the receiver to her breast.

"Immediately."

She glared angrily at him. Not everyone was accustomed to his pace. She was tired, hungry, and not in the most congenial mood.

"Will you be requiring my services?" She didn't bother to hide the resentment in her voice.

"Naturally, I'll need you to translate for me."

"Do you mind if I eat something first?" she asked as she reached for her shoes.

"Yes, I would."

Her gaze narrowed with frustration. "What is it with you? Maybe you can work all hours of the night and day, but others have limitations."

His mouth thinned, revealing his irritation; he picked up his cane. "Then stay."

As much as she would have liked to do exactly that, Stephanie couldn't. Reluctantly she followed him. "Miss Coulter—" she mimicked his low voice sarcastically "—you've done a wonderful job today. Let me express my deepest appreciation. You deserve a break." She paused to eye him. The stone mask was locked tightly in place. "Why, thank you, Mr. Lockwood. Everyone needs a few words of encouragement now and then, and you seem to know just when I need them most. It's been a long grueling day, but those few words of appreciation seem to have made everything worthwhile."

"Are you through, Miss Coulter?" he asked sharply as they stepped into the elevator.

"Quite through." Her back was stiff and straight as they descended. She was tired, her feet ached, and she was hungry. For the last eleven hours, she'd been at his beck and call. What more could he possibly expect from her now? Apparently she was soon to discover the answer.

The driver was waiting outside the hotel when they approached. He held open the door, and Stephanie climbed inside. Jonas paused to speak to the driver, but what he said and whether the driver understood him didn't concern her at the moment. If he needed her to translate, he'd ask. Asking was something Jonas had no problem doing.

They'd gone only a few blocks when the driver pulled to the curb and parked. They were in front of an elegant restaurant. Tiny tables were set outside the door, and white-coated waiters with red cloths draped over their forearms stood in attendance, watching for the smallest hint of a request. Stephanie blinked twice. Exhausted and dispirited, she didn't know if she could bear another meeting now. As it was, her stomach would growl through the entire affair.

"Well, Miss Coulter," Jonas said, climbing agilely out of the car. "I did hear you say you were hungry, right?"

Stunned, Stephanie didn't move. "We're dining here?"

"That is, unless you have any objections?" He suddenly looked bored with the entire process.

"No... I'm starved."

"I believe you've already stated as much. I have a reservation, unless you'd prefer eating in the car."

"I'm coming." This was almost too good to be true. Eagerly she made her way onto the pavement. As they walked into the plush interior, Stephanie's gaze fell longingly on an empty table outside the restaurant.

Jonas surprised her by asking, "Would you prefer to dine outside?"

"Yes, I'd like that."

Jonas spoke to the maître d', who led them to the table and politely held out Stephanie's chair for her. He handed each of them a menu. She was so hungry that her gaze quickly scanned the contents. "Oh, I do love vichyssoise," she said aloud, biting into her lower lip.

Before she knew what was happening, Jonas had attracted the waiter's attention and gestured with his hands. "A bowl of vichyssoise for the lady."

"Jonas," she said, shocked. "Why did you do that?"

"From the way you were acting, I was afraid you were about to keel over from hunger."

"I am," she admitted, her gaze going up one side of the menu and down the other. "Everything looks wonderful."

"What would you like?"

"I can't decide between a huge spinach salad or a whole chicken."

The waiter returned, hands behind his back as he inquired courteously if they'd like to place their orders. Jonas asked for the bouillabaisse, and raised questioning eyes to Stephanie.

"I'll have one of those," she said, pointing to the tray another waiter was delivering. A huge salad was piled high with fresh pink shrimp. "And one of those." Her gaze flew across the room to the dessert tray spread thick with a variety of scrumptious, calorie-laden goodies.

"Will that be all?"

"Oh heavens, yes." She felt guilty enough already. "This is what you get for depriving me of nourishment," she joked. "I'm a grouch when I get too hungry."

"I hadn't noticed." One side of his mouth lifted in an action that appeared aloofly mocking.

"I guess I owe you an apology for what I said earlier."

Her soup arrived, and she eagerly dipped her spoon into it, closing her eyes at the heavenly flavor. "Oh, this is absolutely wonderful. Thank you, Jonas."

His eyes smiled into hers. "You're quite welcome."

"I am sorry."

"My dear Stephanie, I've stopped counting the times you've let your mouth outdistance your mind."

Stephanie was so shocked that her spoon was poised halfway between the bowl and her mouth. Jonas joking! Jonas calling her *dear*! It was almost more than her numbed mind could assimilate.

No sooner had she finished the soup than the salad was delivered. The top was thick with shrimp. "I think I've died and gone to heaven."

"Then you're relatively easy to please. It was my understanding that women were more interested in diamonds and furs."

Stephanie eagerly stabbed her fork into a shrimp. "I haven't eaten one of those in months!"

Jonas arched two thick eyebrows expressively. "So a man could win you over with cheesecake."

"Tonight he could." Unable to wait any longer, she ate the fat shrimp and closed her eyes at the scrumptious flavor. When she opened them, she discovered that Jonas was watching her. Tiny laugh lines fanned out from his eyes.

He was so handsome that Stephanie couldn't take her eyes from him. "Are you wooing me?" It seemed overwhelmingly important that she know where she stood with Jonas.

"I will admit you're the cheapest date I've had in a long time."

"Is this a date?"

"Think of it more as a token of appreciation for a job well done."

Stephanie pressed her hand dramatically to her forehead, and her bright blue eyes grew round with feigned shock. "Do my ears deceive me? The Jonas Lockwood of Lockwood Industries finds a woman of value? A relatively young woman at that—one with faults."

"You won't have me disagreeing with you there."

Despite herself, Stephanie laughed. "No, I don't suppose you would."

"You did very well today."

"Thank you." She felt inexplicably humble.

"Where did you learn to speak French?"

He seemed to want to keep the conversation going, and Stephanie was just as eager to comply. For the first time since meeting the man, she didn't feel on guard around him.

"My grandmother was a French war bride, and she taught my mother the language as a child. Later, Mom majored in French at the University of Washington. I've been bilingual almost from the day I was born."

"You're from Washington State?"

"Colville. Ever hear of it?"

"I can't say that I have."

"Don't worry, most people haven't."

"I imagine you were the town's beauty queen."

"Not me. In fact, I was a tall, skinny kid with buckteeth and knobby knees most of my life. It wasn't until I was in my late teens and the braces came off that the boys noticed me."

"I have trouble believing that."

"It's true." She reached for her purse, and took out her billfold. "I carry this picture because people don't believe me." She withdrew it from her wallet, and was about to hand it to him when they were interrupted by the waiter.

Seeming annoyed, Jonas looked up and spoke briefly with the other man.

Stephanie's blue eyes widened with astonishment and surprise. The waiter nodded and stepped away.

"You speak French."

"Only a little."

"But well."

"Thank you." He dipped his head, accepting her compliment.

A clenching sensation attacked her stomach. "You didn't really need me at all, did you?"

Chapter Four

I brought you along as a translator," Jonas answered simply.

Stephanie lowered her fork to her plate. Her thoughts were churning like water left to boil too long, bubbling and spitting out scalding thoughts she would have preferred to keep in her subconscious. He'd tricked her into accompanying him on this trip—for what reason she could only guess. The meal that had tasted like ambrosia only seconds before felt like a concrete block in the pit of her stomach. "You speak fluent French."

"My French is adequate," Jonas countered, reaching for his wineglass.

"It's as articulate as my own."

"My dear Ms. Coulter, my linguistic abilities have nothing to do with the reason I brought you to France."

"Then why..." She couldn't understand the man. One minute he was personable and considerate, and the next he became brusque and arrogant. The transformation was made with such ease that Stephanie hardly knew how to respond to him.

"That I required a translator is all you need to know."

Rather than argue with him further, Stephanie forked another plump shrimp. She ate it slowly, but for all the enjoyment it gave her she might as well have been chewing on rubber. "Letting the French company we're negotiating with believe you didn't speak the language is all part of your strategy, isn't it?"

"Wine?" Jonas lifted the long-necked green bottle a waiter had recently delivered and motioned to her with it.

"Jonas?"

He cocked his head to one side and nodded. "I can see you're learning."

Stephanie ate another pink shrimp, and discovered that some of the flavor had returned. "You devil!"

"Stephanie, business is business."

"And what is this?" The chardonnay was excellent, and she took another sip, studying him as she tilted the narrow glass to her lips.

He stiffened. "What do you mean?"

"Our dinner. Is it business or pleasure?"

The crow's-feet at the corners of Jonas's eyes fanned out as if he were smiling, yet his mouth revealed not a trace of amusement. "A little of both, I suspect."

"Then I'm honored. I would have assumed that you'd prefer to escort a much more *mature* woman to dinner." She felt the laughter slide up her throat, but suppressed it with some difficulty. "Someone far less emotional than a *younger* woman."

"I believe it was you who commented that age has little to do with maturity."

"*Touché*, Jonas, *touché*." Stephanie raised her wineglass in salute and sipped the wine to toast his wit. She felt light-headed and mellow, but wasn't sure what was to blame: Jonas, her fatigue, or the excellent wine.

She couldn't believe this was happening. The two of them together, enjoying each other's company, bantering like old friends, applauding each other's skill. She imagined that Jonas was about as relaxed as he ever allowed himself to be. As little as two hours ago, she would have thought it impossible to carry on a civil conversation with the man.

"I'll admit that the pleasure part comes from the fact I knew you wouldn't be simpering at my feet," Jonas commented, breaking into her thoughts.

"I never simper."

"You much prefer to challenge and bully."

"Bully? Me?" She laughed a little and shook her head. "I guess maybe I do at that, but just a bit." She didn't like admitting it, but he was right. She was the oldest of three girls, and did have a tendency to take matters into her own hands. "While we're on the subject of bullies, I don't suppose you've noticed the way *you* treat people?"

"We weren't discussing me," he said dryly.

"We most certainly are." She flattened her palms on either side of her plate and shook her head, unwilling to alter the course of the conversation. "I've never known anyone who treats people the way you do. What I can't understand is how you command such loyalty."

He arched both eyebrows expressively, and his mocking gaze swept her with mocking thoroughness.

Stephanie ignored him, and continued. "It's more than just money. You pay well, but the benefits leave a lot to be desired." She mentioned this because the girls from the office had.

"Is that a fact?"

"You're often unreasonable." She knew she was pressing her luck, but the wine had mellowed her.

"Perhaps," he admitted reluctantly. "But only when the occasion calls for it."

For all the heed he paid her comments, they could have been discussing the traffic. "And I've yet to mention your outrageous temper."

"I wasn't aware that I had a temper."

"You demand as much from your staff as you do yourself."

"As every employer should."

Despite the fact he didn't seem to find their conversation the least bit amusing, Stephanie continued. "But by far, the very worst of your faults is your overactive imagination."

His gaze flew to hers and narrowed. "What makes you suggest something so absurd?"

Stephanie knew she'd trapped him, and she loved having the upper hand for the first time in their short acquaintance. "You actually believed I was meeting someone last night."

"With your own mouth you admitted as much."

Stephanie nearly choked on her wine; her gaze captured and challenged his. "I most certainly did no such thing."

"You mentioned the taxi driver—"

"That's so farfetched, I can't believe you'd stoop that low."

"Perhaps, but you seemed to have enjoyed yourself. You spoke at length of the sights you'd seen."

"If you want the truth, I hardly saw a thing. I was thinking about—" She stopped herself in the nick of time from admitting that her thoughts had been filled with him.

"Yes?" Jonas prompted.

"I was preoccupied with the meeting today...I was worried about how I'd do."

"Your French is superb. You needn't have been anxious, and you know it. What *did* occupy your thoughts? Or should I say who?"

Stephanie was saved from answering by the waiter, who reappeared to take their plates. She gave him a grateful smile and finished the last of her wine before the man returned with two steaming cups of coffee.

Jonas asked for the bill, paused and looked at Stephanie. "Unless you'd like something more? Another dessert, perhaps?"

"No." She shook her head for emphasis and placed her hands over her stomach. After downing half of everything on the menu, she felt badly in need of exercise.

The sun had set, and the sky was darkening in shades of pink by the time they finished the last of their coffee.

"Shall we go?"

Stephanie nodded and stood. "Everything was wonderful. Thank you." The food had been marvelous; she freely admitted that, but it was this time with Jonas that had made the dinner so right. For this brief span of time, they hadn't sharpened their claws at the other's expense. Stephanie didn't want the evening to end. For the first time since she'd worked with Jonas, she felt at ease with him. She feared that once they arrived back at the hotel, everything would revert to the way it had always been between them. Jonas would immerse himself in the papers Adam was getting for him, and everything would be business, business, business.

The maître d' was about to call for the limousine when Stephanie placed her hand on Jonas's arm. "Would you mind if we walked a bit?"

"Not at all." Jonas turned toward the maître d', who nodded and wished them a pleasant evening.

"I ate so much that I feel like a stuffed turkey at Thanksgiving. I'm sure a little exercise will help." She was conscious of his leg, but trusted that if it pained him, he would say something. His limp was barely noticeable as they strolled down the narrow sidewalk. "There's a park across the way."

"That sounds perfect."

They crossed the street and sauntered down the paved walkway that led them into the lush green lawns of a city park. Black wrought-iron fences bordered flower beds filled with bright red tulips and yellow crocuses. Row upon row of trees welcomed them, proudly displaying their buds with the promise of new life.

"I've always heard Paris in springtime couldn't be equaled," Stephanie said softly. She mused that anyone happening upon them would think they were lovers. Paris in the spring was said to be a city meant for lovers. For tonight she'd pretend—reality would crowd in on her soon enough.

They followed the walkway that led to the center of the park, where a tall fountain spilled water from the mouths of circling lions' heads.

"Shall we make a wish?" she asked, feeling happy and excited.

Jonas snorted softly. "Why waste good money?"

"Don't be such a skeptic. It's traditional to throw a coin in a fountain, any fountain, and what better place than Paris for wishes to come true?" She opened her purse, digging for loose change. "Here, it's my treat." She handed him a dime, since she had little French money with her.

"You don't honestly expect me to fall victim to such stupidity?"

"Humor me, Jonas." She noted the amusement in his blue eyes, and she ignored his tone, which sounded harsh and disapproving.

"All right." Without aim or apparent premeditation, he tossed the dime into the water with as much ceremony as if he were throwing something into the garbage.

"Good grief," Stephanie muttered beneath her breath. "I don't know of a single fairy in the entire universe who would honor such a wish."

"Why not?" he demanded.

"You obviously haven't given the matter much thought."

One corner of his mouth edged upward slightly. "I was humoring you, remember?"

"Did you even make a wish?"

He shrugged. "Not exactly."

"Well, no wonder." She shook her head dolefully and looked at him in mock disdain. "Try it again, and this time be a little more sincere."

His eyes revealed exactly what he thought of this exercise. Nonetheless, Jonas reached inside his own pocket and took out a silver dollar.

Stephanie's hand stopped him. "That's too much."

"It's a big wish." His look was far more thoughtful as he took aim and sent the coin skipping over the surface of the water. The silver dollar made a small splash before sinking into the whirling depths.

Stephanie gave him a brilliant smile. "Okay, my turn." She turned her back to the fountain, rubbed the nickel between her palms to warm it, closed her eyes and, with all the reverence due magical wish-granting fairies, flung the coin over her shoulder and into the fountain. "There," she said, satisfied.

"How long?" Jonas demanded.

"How long for what?"

"How long," he repeated with exasperation, "must one wait before the wish comes true?"

"It depends on what you wished for." She made it sound as though she had accumulated all the knowledge there was on the subject. "Certain wishes require a bit of manipulating by the forces that be. However, I'm only familiar with wishes made in American fountains. Things could be much different here. It could be that the wish fairies who guard this fountain are on a slower time scale than elsewhere."

"I see." It was clear from the frown that dented his brow that he didn't.

"Maybe you should just tell me what you wished for," Stephanie suggested next, "and I can give you an estimate of the approximate time you'll have to wait for your wish."

"It's my understanding that one must never reveal one's wish."

"That's not true anymore." Stephanie laughed, enjoying their inane discussion. "Science has proved that theory to be inaccurate."

"Oh?"

"Yes, I'm surprised you didn't read about it."

"So am I." He reached for her hand, and they resumed their walk. "But if that's the case, then perhaps you'd be willing to share your wish with me."

Color instantly flooded Stephanie's cheeks. She should have known Jonas would turn the tables on her when she least expected it.

"Stephanie?"

It was completely absurd. With everything that was in her she'd wished that Jonas would take her in his arms and kiss her. It was silly and impractical, and as he'd pointed out earlier, a waste of good money.

When she didn't respond immediately, Jonas stopped and turned, standing directly in front of her so that he could look into her eyes.

Stephanie felt the color mount in her face.

"I would think that one who was a self-proclaimed expert on the subject of fountains and wishes would have no qualms about revealing her own wish." He placed his finger under her stubborn chin, elevating her gaze so that she couldn't avoid his.

"I..."

"You still haven't answered my question."

"I wasted the wish on something impractical," she blurted out. The whole park seemed to have gone quiet. Wind ruffled the foliage around them and hissed through the branches, but even the trees seemed to have paused as though they too were interested in her reply. Stephanie swallowed uncomfortably, convinced that Jonas could read her thoughts and that he was silently laughing at her.

"I fear I wasted my wish as well," he informed her softly.

"You did?" Her eyes sought his for the first time.

He placed his hands on each side of her neck at the gentle sloping of her shoulders. "I'm seldom impractical."

"I . . . know."

His mouth descended an inch closer to hers, so close that she could feel his warm breath fanning her face. An inch more and their lips would touch. Stephanie moistened her lips, realizing all at once how very much she wanted to taste his mouth on hers. Her breath froze in her lungs; even her heart stopped beating.

"Could your wish have been as impractical as mine?" There was an unmistakable quaver to his voice.

Stephanie levered her hands against his chest, flattening her palms over his heart. His pulse was strong and even. "Yes." The lone word was breathless and weak, barely audible.

His arms went around her, anchoring her against him. Gently, he laid his cheek alongside hers, rubbing the side of his face over hers as though he feared her touch, yet craved it. Stephanie closed her eyes, savoring his nearness, his warmth and the vital feel of him. A thousand objections shot through her mind, but she refused to listen to even one. This was exactly what she'd wished for at the fountain, fool that she was.

Jonas turned his head and nuzzled her ear with his nose, and she noted his breathing was shallow. His arms tightened around her and he whispered her name, entreating her—for what, Stephanie didn't know.

It was at the back of her mind that she should break free, but something much stronger than the force of her will kept her motionless. He was her employer; they argued constantly and battled with each other at the office. Jonas Lockwood was an arrogant, domineering chauvinist. But all her arguments were burned away like deadwood in a forest fire as his lips moved to her hair. He kissed the top of her head, her cheek, her ear, and then moved back to her hair. He paused, holding her to him as though it were the most natural thing in the world for them to be wrapped in each other's arms.

"Tell me, Stephanie," Jonas asked in a hoarse whisper. "Did you wish for the same thing I did?"

Their eyes met hungrily and locked. Stephanie nodded, unable to answer him with words.

Jonas caught her to him and lowered his mouth to hers, claiming her lips in a greedy kiss that stirred her soul and left her weak and clinging. She felt herself responding; her arms slid around his neck. Their lips clung, and his tongue sought and found hers. Against her will, Stephanie arched against him, seeking to lose herself in his arms for all time.

Abruptly they broke apart, both of their own accord. Stephanie trembled from inside and out. She dared not look at Jonas. Neither spoke. For a moment they didn't move, didn't breathe. The world that only seconds before had been silent now burst into a cacophony of sound. Wind whistled through the trees. Car horns blared from a nearby street. An elderly couple could be heard arguing.

"Jonas, I..."

"Don't say anything."

She wouldn't have known what to say. She was as stunned as he was.

"It was the wine, and this silly wishing business," he said stiffly.

"Right."

"I told you wasting your money on wishes was foolish."

"Exactly," she agreed, though not very strenuously. Their wishes had come true; now they both wanted to complain.

Stephanie noticed on the way out of the park that Jonas seemed to avoid being near her. His steps were quick, rushed. In order to keep up with him, she was forced into a half-run. The instant they hit the main thoroughfare, Jonas raised his hand and hailed the limo that drove them directly back to the hotel.

"Well, how was Paris?" Jan asked the first day Stephanie was back at Lockwood Industries. They sat in the employee cafeteria. Jan had purchased the luncheon special, and Stephanie had brought a sandwich from home.

"Fine."

"Fine?"

"I was held captive in a stuffy, smoke-filled room for most of the four days. This wasn't exactly a vacation, you know."

"How'd you get along with Mr. Lockwood?"

"Fine."

"Is that the only word you know?" Disgruntled, Jan tore open a small bag of potato chips and dumped them on her tray.

"I have an adequate vocabulary."

"Not today, you don't. Come on, Steph, you were with the man day and night for four days. Something must have happened."

The scene by the fountain, when Jonas had held her and kissed her, played back in Stephanie's mind in living Technicolor. If she were to close her eyes, she might be able to feel the pressure of his mouth on hers. She strenuously resisted the urge. "Nothing happened," she lied.

"Then why are you acting so strangely?"

"Am I?" Stephanie focused her attention on her friend, trying to look alert and intelligent even though her thoughts were a thousand miles away in an obscure Paris park.

"You have been acting weird ever since you got back."

"What did you expect would happen?"

"I don't know, but the others thought you might have fallen in love with him."

"Oh, honestly, Jan, you're mistaking jet lag for love."

Disappointment clouded Jan's eyes. "This isn't going well."

"What isn't?"

"This romance. The girls and I had it all planned. We felt it would work out a whole lot easier than it is."

"How do you mean?"

"Well, in the romances, the minute the hero and heroine are alone together for the first time, something usually happens."

"What do you mean, something happens?"

"You know, a kiss in the dark, an intimate dinner for two, a shared smile. Something!"

"We weren't exactly alone; Adam Holmes was with us." She avoided Jan's eyes as she carefully peeled a hard-boiled egg. If Jan could see her eyes, she'd know all. The egg took on new importance as she shucked the shell off piece by piece.

"At any rate," Jan continued, "we'd hoped that things might have taken off between you two."

"I'm sorry to disappoint all of you, but the trip was basically a working arrangement and little else." Stephanie sprinkled salt and pepper on the egg.

"Well, I guess that's it, then."

Stephanie returned the pepper shaker to the holder in the middle of the table. "What do you mean?"

"If Mr. Lockwood was ever going to notice you, it would have been last week. You were constantly in each other's company, even if Adam Holmes was playing the part of legal chaperone. But if Mr. Lockwood isn't attracted to you by now, I doubt that he ever will be."

"I couldn't agree more." Her heart contracted with a pang that felt strangely like disappointment. "Now can I get on with my life? I don't want to hear any more of your corny romance ideas. Understand?"

"All right," Jan agreed, but she didn't look happy about it. "However, I wish you'd start reading romances. You'd understand what we're talking about and play your role a little better."

"Would you stop hounding me with those books? I'm not in the mood for romance."

"Okay, okay, but when you are ready, just say the word."

Stephanie took a look at her untouched egg, sighed, and stuffed it in the sack to toss in the garbage, her appetite gone. She couldn't decide how she felt about

Jonas. Part of her wished the kiss in the park had never happened. Those few minutes had made the remainder of the trip nearly intolerable. Each had taken pains to pretend nothing had happened, going out of their way to be cordial and polite, nothing less and certainly nothing more. It was as if Adam Holmes was their unexpected link with sanity. Neither Jonas nor Stephanie could do without him as they avoided any possibility of being trapped alone together. On the long flight home, Jonas had worked out of his briefcase while Stephanie and Adam played cards. For all the notice Jonas had given her, she could have been a piece of luggage. They'd separated at the airport, and Stephanie hadn't seen Jonas since. It was just as well, she told herself. The incident at the fountain had been a moment out of time, and was best forgotten.

"Steph?"

Stephanie shook her head to free her tangled thoughts. "I'm sorry, were you saying something?"

Jan gave her an odd look. "I was asking if you'd like to meet Jim's cousin, Mark. I thought we might double-date Saturday night. Dinner and a show, that kind of thing."

For a moment, Stephanie couldn't remember who Jim was. "Sure, that sounds like fun." Anything was better than spending another restless weekend alone in her apartment.

"Mark said something about dating again, but I've held him off because I wanted to see how things developed between you and Mr. Lockwood."

Stephanie stared at her blankly and blinked twice, carefully measuring her words. She was saddened by the reality of what she had to say. "It isn't going to work between Jonas and me. Nothing's going to happen." The crazy part was that Stephanie was of two minds on the subject of the company president. He intrigued her. There wasn't a single man who interested her more. He was challenging, intelligent, pigheaded, stubborn, and completely out of her league. Ah well, she thought, sighing expressively, you won some and you lost some. And she'd lost Jonas without ever really having known him.

"Saturday at seven, then?"

"I'll look forward to it." That wasn't stretching the truth all that much. As far as men went, there was little happening in Stephanie's life.

"The three of us will pick you up at your apartment. Okay?"

"That sounds fine."

Jan groaned and laughed. "You're back to that word again."

Saturday evening, Stephanie washed her hair and spent extra time coiling it into a long braid that reached the middle of her back. The trick was one that her sister had taught her. She dressed casually in cords and a bulky knit sweater her mother had sent her last Christmas. The winter-wheat color reminded her of the rolling hills of grain outside her hometown.

The doorbell chimed, and Stephanie expelled her breath forcefully. She wasn't looking forward to this evening. All day her thoughts had drifted back to Jonas and their time in Paris, especially their stroll in the park. If she went out with anyone tonight, she wanted it to be with him. Wishful thinking, and not a fountain in sight! She wasn't especially eager to meet Jim's cousin either. Jan had tried to build him up, but Stephanie knew from experience the problems that could be encountered on a blind date. Had she had her wits about her and been less concerned about revealing her attraction to Jonas, she would have declined the invitation. But it was too late now.

She needn't have worried about Mark. He looked nice enough, although it came out in the first couple of minutes that he was newly divorced. Miserable, too, judging from the look in his eyes.

The vivacious Jan carried the conversation once the introductions were finished with.

"Would anyone like some wine before we leave?" The tray with the wine glasses was set up on the coffee table, waiting for their arrival. "It's a light white wine."

"Sounds marvelous," Jan said, linking her fingers with Jim's. The two claimed the sofa and sat side by side. Mark took a chair, leaving its twin for Stephanie.

Still standing, she poured the wine. "What movie are we seeing?"

"There's a new foreign film out that sounds interesting."

The doorbell chimed, and Stephanie got up to answer it. "I'm not expecting anyone," she announced to her guests. "It's probably the paperboy wanting to collect." The youth seemed to do so at the most inopportune times. Last month she'd been in the shower shampooing her hair when he'd come.

Undoing the lock, Stephanie was about to tease the teenager about his bad timing when she stopped cold. It wasn't the paperboy who stood on the other side of her door; it was Jonas Lockwood.

Chapter Five

Jonas." Stephanie experienced a sense of joy so strong she nearly choked on it. Just when she'd given up any hope of seeing him again, he'd come to her. But her joy quickly turned to regret as she heard Jan, Jim and Mark talking behind her. "What are you doing here?" she whispered fiercely.

Jonas stood stiffly on the other side of the door, his expression impossible to read. His grip on his cane tightened. "I came to see you."

Jan apparently heard Stephanie's exclamation of surprise and murmured something to Jim about Stephanie and Jonas.

"May I come in?" Jonas asked.

"Yes...of course. I didn't mean to be rude." She stepped aside, her hand still holding the doorknob. Jonas's timing couldn't have been worse, but she was so pleased to see him that she wouldn't have cared if he'd arrived unannounced on Christmas Eve.

"Mr. Lockwood, how nice to see you again," Jan said, tossing Stephanie a knowing look that was capable of translating whole foreign libraries.

Both Jim and Mark stood, and Stephanie made awkward introductions. "Jim, Mark, this is Mr. Lockwood."

"Jonas," he said, correcting her and offering them his hand.

"Would you care for a glass of wine?" Jan offered.

"Yes, please," Stephanie hurried to add, her face filling with color at her lack of good manners. The heat threatened to suffocate her cheeks with its warmth. "Please stay and have some wine." Before he could answer, she walked into the kitchen for another wineglass, filled it and handed it to Jonas, who had claimed the chair next to Mark.

Resisting the urge to press her cool hands against her flaming cheeks, Stephanie took a seat on the sofa beside Jan. The men were asking Jonas questions about the business of manufacturing small parts for airplane engines as though it was the most interesting topic in the world. Jonas answered each question with the same seriousness with which it was asked. While the men were occupied, Jan took the opportunity to jab Stephanie in the ribs with her elbow. "I thought you said he wasn't interested," she whispered under her breath.

"He isn't," Stephanie insisted. Glancing around, Stephanie wanted to groan with frustration. Although the small, one-bedroom apartment suited her nicely, Stephanie was intensely conscious that most of her furniture was secondhand and well-worn. She hadn't been the least bit ashamed to have Jan and her friends view her mix-and-match arrangement, but entertaining Jonas Lockwood was another matter entirely. Oh, for heaven's sake, what did she care? He hadn't stopped by to check out her china pattern.

"I can see that I've come at a bad time," Jonas said, standing. He set his glass aside, and Stephanie noted that he hadn't bothered to taste the wine.

Stephanie stood with him.

"We were about to leave for dinner," Jan explained apologetically. "But if you needed Steph for something at the office, we could change our plans."

"That won't be necessary." He shook hands with Jim and Mark a second time. "It was a pleasure meeting you both."

"I'll walk you to the door," Stephanie offered, locking her fingers together in front of her. He'd stopped in out of the blue, and she wasn't about to let him escape without knowing the reason for his impromptu visit.

Instead of stopping to ask him at her front door, Stephanie stepped outside into the hall with him. For a moment, neither spoke. Stephanie was trying to come up with a subtle way of mentioning that she'd only met Mark a few minutes before, that the blind date had been Jan's idea, and that she'd only fallen into it because she didn't think that Jonas wanted to see her again. But she couldn't explain without looking like a fool.

"I apologize for not calling first," Jonas said finally.

"It...doesn't matter. I'm almost always home."

He cocked his brow as though he didn't quite believe her.

"It's true."

He glanced at his wristwatch. "I must be going."

"Jonas." Her hands were clenched so tightly that she was sure she'd cut off the blood supply to her fingers. "Why did you come?"

"It isn't important."

It was terribly important to her. "Is it something from the office?"

"No."

"Then . . . why?"

"I believe there's a young man in there waiting for you. I consider it poor manners for you to remain in this hallway with me, discussing my motives."

"What is this? Do you want to play twenty questions?"

He frowned.

"All right, you obviously want me to guess the reason you stopped by. Fine. Since that's the way you want it, let's start with the basics. Is it animal, vegetable or mineral?"

"Ms. Coulter." He closed his eyes, seemingly frustrated by her tenacity.

"I'm not going back inside until you tell me why you're here."

"This is neither the time nor the place to discuss it." His gaze hardened.

The look was one Stephanie knew all too well. "It's common courtesy to tell someone why you stopped by."

"The only manners you need concern yourself with are your own toward your friends. Now I suggest that you join them. We can discuss this later."

"When?" She wasn't about to let him off as easily as that.

"Monday."

She didn't want to agree, but she could hear the others talking and knew they'd long since finished their wine. "All right, I'll wait until Monday."

His gaze rested on her for a long moment. "It would be far better if you forgot I was ever here."

"I'm not going to do that." How could she? She hadn't been so pleased to see anyone in months.

"I didn't think you would. Enjoy yourself tonight." He said it with such sincerity that she wanted to assure him that she would, even though she knew the entire evening was a waste.

"Goodbye, Jonas."

"Goodbye." He looped the end of his cane over his forearm and turned away from her.

Stephanie watched him go, biting into her lower lip to keep from calling him back. If there had been any decent way of doing so, she would have sent Jan, Jim and Mark on their way without her. Reluctantly, she went back inside her apartment.

As she had known it would be, the evening was time misspent. Mark's conversation consisted of an account of the wrongs committed by his ex-wife and of talking about how terribly he missed his children. Stephanie tried to appear sympathetic, but her thoughts were centered on Jonas. They wavered between quiet jubilation and heart-wrenching despair. More than once, she had to resist the urge to tell Mark to be quiet and go back to his wife since it was so obvious that he still loved her. A thousand times over she wished she'd never agreed to this blind date, and silently vowed she wouldn't do it again, no matter how close the friend who arranged it. Stephanie hoped Jan appreciated what she was going through, but somehow she doubted it.

After the movie, the foursome returned to Stephanie's apartment for coffee. Jan offered to help as an excuse to talk to her alone.

"Well, what do you think?"

"Mark's nice, but he's in love with his wife."

"Not about Mark. I'm talking about Mr. Lockwood...Jonas," she said correcting herself. "I knew it. From the first, I knew. Lordy, girl, he's hooked!"

"Oh, hardly. Mr. Lockwood has no feelings for me one way or the other." She filled the basket with coffee and slipped it into place above the glass pot with unnecessary force.

"Don't give me that," Jan countered sharply. "I saw the way you two were looking at each other."

"I don't even know why he came." She busied herself opening and closing cupboards and taking down four matching cups.

"Don't be such a dope. There's only one reason he showed up. He wanted to see you again. He's interested with a capital *I*." Jan crossed her arms and leaned indolently against the back of the kitchen counter. "He's so enthralled with you that he can't look at you without letting it show."

"You're exaggerating again." Stephanie prayed her friend was right, but she sincerely doubted it. Jonas Lockwood wasn't the kind of man to reveal his emotions as freely as that.

"I'm not exaggerating."

"Come on," Stephanie said, refusing to argue, "the guys are waiting."

"Just do me a favor."

"What now?" Stephanie cried, desperate to change the subject. It was bad enough that Jonas had dominated her thoughts all evening. Now Jan was bringing him up as well.

"Just think about it. Jonas Lockwood wouldn't have stopped by here for any reason other than the fact that he wanted to see you."

Jan's logic was irrefutable, but Stephanie still wasn't sure she could believe it. "All right, I'll think about it, but for heaven's sake don't tell anyone. The last thing I need is Maureen and the rest to find out about this."

"I won't breathe a word of it." But Jan's eyes were twinkling. "I'll give you some time to think things through. You're smart; you'll figure Lockwood out." Jan held the door open for Stephanie, who carried the tray with the four steaming cups of coffee into the living room.

After a half hour of strained conversation, mostly about Mark's ex-wife, Jan and friends departed. Stephanie sighed as she let them out the door. It was only eleven, but Stephanie hurriedly got ready for bed. Yet, for all the doubts and uncertainty she faced regarding Jonas, she slept surprisingly well.

Sunday morning, Jan was at Stephanie's front door, smiling broadly and carrying a large stack of romances under one arm.

"What are those for?" Stephanie asked, letting her friend into the apartment. She was still in her housecoat, fighting off a cold with orange juice and aspirin, and feeling guilty for being so lazy.

"Not what—who."

"All right. Who are those for?" Her sore throat had taken a lot of the fight out of her.

"You."

"Jan, I've told you repeatedly that I'm not into romances. You can't force me to read them."

"No, but I thought you might be interested in a little research." She paused, noticing Stephanie's appearance for the first time. "What's the matter—are you sick?"

"No, I'm just fighting off a cold." And maybe a touch of disappointment, too.

"Great, there's no better time to sit back and read."

"Jan..."

Her friend held up her hand to stop her. "I refuse to hear any arguments. I want you to sit down and read. If I have to, I'll stand over you until you do."

Muttering under her breath, Stephanie complied, sitting on the sofa with her back against the armrest and bringing her feet up so she could tuck them under a blanket. Jan picked up the romance on the top of the pile, silently read the back cover and nodded knowingly. "You'll like this one. The circumstances are similar to what's happening between you and Mr. Lockwood."

Stephanie bolted to her feet. "Nothing's happening between me and Mr. Lockwood."

"You called him Jonas the other day," Jan said, ignoring Stephanie's bad mood. "The funny part is, I know that I'll never be able to think of him other than as *Mr.* Lockwood."

To the contrary, Stephanie had always thought of him as Jonas, but she wasn't about to add ammunition to her friend's growing arsenal.

"But I don't think we need worry about his name."

"Thank heaven for that much," Stephanie muttered, sitting back down.

"Promise me you'll read these?"

"I would never have taken you for such an unreasonable slave driver." She fought back a flash of mutinous pride and shook her head. "All right, I'll read, but I won't like it."

"And I bet you a month's wages you'll end up loving them the way the rest of us do."

"I'm reserving judgment."

Jan left soon after Stephanie opened the cover of the first book. To be honest, she was curious what Jan, Toni, Maureen and Barbara saw in the books that they read with such fervor. What was even more interesting was the fact that these women did more than just read the books; the whole group talked about the characters as though they were living, breathing people. Stephanie had once heard Barbara comment that she'd like to punch a certain hero out, and the others had agreed wholeheartedly, as though it was entirely possible to do so.

The next time Stephanie glanced at the clock, it was afternoon and she'd finished the first book, astonished at how well-written it was. All along she'd assumed that romance heroines were sappy, weak-willed chits without a brain in their heads. From tidbits of information she'd heard among the other women, she couldn't imagine anyone putting up with some of the things the heroines in the books did. But she was wrong. The woman in the first romance she read and the one she reached for next were modern women with modern problems that they faced on an adult level. Although Stephanie might not have agreed completely with the way the heroines handled their relationships with their heroes, she appreciated why they acted the way they did. With love, she realized, came tolerance, acceptance and understanding.

* * *

First thing on Monday morning, Stephanie stopped at Jan's desk in personnel. She dutifully placed the three romances in Jan's Out basket, willing to admit that she had misjudged Jan's favorite reading material.

"What's that for?"

"I read them."

"And?" Jan's eyes grew round.

"I loved them, just the way you said I would."

Laughing, Jan nodded, reached for her phone and punched out Maureen's extension. "She read the first three and she's hooked." Once she'd made her announcement, she replaced the receiver and sat back, folding her hands neatly on top of the desk and sighing. "I'm waiting."

Stephanie groaned and shook her head lightly. "I knew I wasn't going to get away this easily. You want to hear it—all right, all right—you told me so."

Jan laughed again. "You look especially nice today. Any reason?"

Stephanie considered a white lie, but quickly changed her mind. Like the heroines in the romances, she was an adult woman, and if she happened to be attracted to a man, it wasn't a sin to admit as much. "I'll be talking to Jonas later, and I wanted to look my best."

"You'll keep me up to date, won't you?"

Stephanie secured the strap of her purse on her shoulder. "I don't know that there'll be anything to report. Our relationship isn't like those romances."

"Maybe not yet, but it will be," Jan said with the utmost confidence.

"I'm not half as convinced as you are. Just keep this under your hat. I don't want the others to know."

"My lips are sealed."

But Stephanie wondered if Jan was capable of keeping anything a secret. Her co-worker was much too friendly, and much too eager to see something develop between Stephanie and Jonas.

The day went smoothly although Stephanie was constantly on edge, expecting to hear from Jonas. Each time her phone rang, she felt certain it would be the company president, issuing a request to have her join him in his office. He didn't call, and by five o'clock Stephanie felt both disappointed and frustrated. Jonas had said he'd talk to her on Monday, and she'd taken him at his word.

Jan, Toni, Maureen and Barbara sauntered in together at quitting time. "Well? What did he say?"

Stephanie glared at Jan, who quickly lowered her eyes. "I couldn't help it," she murmured, looking miserable. "Toni guessed, and I couldn't lie."

"You didn't have any problem promising me your lips were sealed."

"She had to tell us," Maureen insisted. "It was our right. We're the ones who got you into this."

Stephanie straightened the papers on the corner of her desk. "I'm not sure I can find it in my heart to thank you. Jonas Lockwood has been a thorn in my side from the moment we met."

"Perfect," Barbara announced, her head bobbing once.

"Enough of that. We want to know what he had to say today."

"Nothing." Stephanie tried unsuccessfully to hide the disappointment in her voice.

"Nothing!" the others echoed.

"I haven't seen him."

"Why not?"

"Good grief, how am I to know?"

Toni paused, and pressed her forefinger to her temple. "You know, in mulling over the events of Saturday night, I don't think it was necessarily such a bad thing that Jan's friend was there with Stephanie. It lets Mr. Lockwood know that he's got some competition."

"It may be just enough to scare him off, though," Barbara disagreed.

"Then he isn't worth his salt as a hero."

"Would you four stop!" Stephanie demanded, waving her arms for emphasis. She returned her attention to Jan. "Are they always like this?"

Jan shrugged. "What are you going to do?"

Stephanie hadn't given the matter very much thought. Jonas had said that he'd talk to her Monday, and several hours remained in the day. It could be that his intentions were to contact her at her apartment. Stephanie quickly dismissed the notion. He wouldn't be back; she'd seen it in his eyes.

"Steph?"

She looked up to notice that all four of her coworkers were studying her expectantly.

"I'm going to his office," she said, the announcement shocking her as much as it did the others. The upper floor belonged to Jonas and was well guarded by his secretary, Bertha Westheimer, who was reputed to have slain more than one persistent dragon.

Jan made an O with her thumb and index finger and shook her head. "Didn't I tell you she was heroine material?"

"The perfect choice," Maureen agreed.

The four of them followed Stephanie out of her office and to the elevator. Barbara pushed the button for her. Toni and Maureen stood behind her, rubbing her shoulders as though to prepare her for the coming confrontation. For a moment, Stephanie felt as if she was preparing for the heavyweight boxing championship of the world.

"Don't take any guff from Old Stone Face."

"Just remember to smile at Mr. Lockwood."

"And it wouldn't hurt to bat those baby blues a time or two."

Armed with this excellent advice, Stephanie entered the waiting elevator. Jan gave her the thumbs-up sign just before the heavy metal doors closed.

Now that she was alone, Stephanie felt herself losing her nerve. She sighed and leaned against the back of the elevator. The others had lent her confidence, but standing alone in the chilly, dimly lit elevator gave her cause to doubt. If there had been any way of disappearing from a moving elevator, Stephanie would have been tempted to try it.

The doors opened, and Bertha Westheimer raised her eyes to frown at Stephanie's approach. A pair of glasses were delicately balanced at the end of her nose. She was near forty, Stephanie guessed, tall and slender, with a narrow mouth. Just looking at the woman inspired fear.

"Do you have an appointment?" Bertha asked stiffly, giving Stephanie a look that was not at all welcoming.

Stephanie stepped off the elevator and thrust back her shoulders, prepared for this first encounter. "Mr.

Lockwood asked to see me." That was only a partial white lie.

"Your name, please?" With the eraser end of her pencil, Bertha flipped through the appointment schedule.

"Stephanie Coulter."

"I don't see your name down here, Ms. Coulter."

"Then there must be some mistake."

There was challenge in Bertha's dark brown eyes. "I don't make mistakes."

"Then I suggest you contact Mr. Lockwood."

"I'll do exactly that." Jonas's secretary sat in her upholstered chair and flipped on the intercom. "There's a Ms. Coulter here to see you. She claims she has an appointment." There was enough lilt in her voice to suggest that Stephanie had lied.

"I said," Stephanie corrected her through clenched teeth, "that Mr. Lockwood had asked to see me." The hand clenching her purse tightened. "There's a difference."

The silence on the other end of the intercom stretched out uncomfortably, and Stephanie was convinced she was about to be dismissed.

"Mr. Lockwood?"

"Send her in, Miss Westheimer."

Stephanie flashed Jonas's guardian a brilliant smile of triumph as she waltzed past her desk. The older woman had to know that Stephanie had been her replacement while she was ill, yet she gave no indication that she was aware who Stephanie was, or even that she was employed by Lockwood Industries.

Stephanie let herself into Jonas's office and was instantly met by a rush of memories. She liked this room, just as she respected the man who ruled from it.

Jonas was busy writing, his head bowed, and didn't bother to acknowledge her presence. Stephanie stood awkwardly as she waited for him to finish, not enough at ease to take a seat without being asked.

When he'd finished, Jonas put the cap on his pen and set it aside before glancing in her direction. "Yes?"

His crisp tone made her all the more uncomfortable. "You said you would talk to me on Monday."

"About?"

He was making this difficult; she drew in a deep breath before continuing. "About Saturday night. You told me we'd talk."

"I don't recall committing myself to that."

"Please, don't play games with me. You stopped by my apartment on Saturday, and I want to know why."

The lines around his mouth deepened, but he wasn't smiling. "I happened to be in the neighborhood."

"But..."

"Leave it at that, Ms. Coulter. It was a mistake, and one best forgotten."

"But I didn't think it was a mistake." He was closing her out; she could see it by the way he sat, his back stiff with determination. His eyes looked past her as though he wanted to avoid seeing her.

The silence was broken by Jonas. "Sometimes it's better to leave things as they are. In my opinion, this is one of those times."

Her hands trembled slightly but she stood her ground. "I disagree."

His mouth twisted in a cynical smile. "Unfortunately, you have little say in the matter. Now, if you'll excuse me, I have several papers to read over."

It was clearly meant to be a dismissal, and Stephanie wavered indecisively between stalking out of the office and trying to forget Jonas and staying and admitting that she was attracted to him and that she'd like to know him better. But for all the attention he was giving her now, she might as well have been a stack of signed papers on his desk. Out of sight, out of mind, she mused ruefully. Her pride told her that she had better things to do than allow Jonas Lockwood to poke holes in her fragile ego.

Finally her pride won, and she gave him a small, sad smile. "You don't need to be rude, Jonas. I get the message."

"Do you?" He focused his gaze on her.

"Thank you for that wonderful night in Paris. I'll remember that and you fondly."

His hard blue eyes softened. "Stephanie, listen..."

He was interrupted by the phone. "I'm waiting for a call," he said, almost apologetically, as he reached for the receiver.

Stephanie turned to leave, but Jonas stopped her as he reverted to French. Stephanie could tell that he was speaking to a government official regarding his contract with Lockwood Industries' French counterpart, but the conversation became too technical for Stephanie to understand fully.

Ten minutes later, Jonas hung up the telephone. His eyes revealed his excitement.

"Congratulations are in order," he said, coming to a stand. "Our trip to France was a success. By the beginning of the year, there will be a ground-breaking ceremony for the first foreign site of Lockwood Industries."

"Congratulations," Stephanie whispered. His happiness was contagious; it filled the enormous room, encircling them both.

Jonas walked around the front of the large rosewood desk, his eyes sparkling. "It seemed for a while that this deal could go either way."

Stephanie noticed that his limp was less pronounced now than at any time she'd seen him walk.

"Do you know what this means?" He walked to the other side of the carpet, as though he couldn't contain himself any longer.

Stephanie nodded eagerly, pretending she did know when in actuality she was ignorant of nearly all the pertinent information.

His hands locked on her shoulders. "I can't believe it's falling into place after all the problems we've encountered." His arms dropped to her waist and circled her. With a burst of infectious laughter, he lifted her off the plush carpet and swung her around.

Caught completely off guard, Stephanie gasped and placed her hands on his shoulders in an effort to maintain her balance. "I'm very pleased for you."

As if suddenly aware that he was holding her, Jonas relaxed his grip. Stephanie's feet found the floor, but her hands remained on his shoulders, and her eyes smiled warmly into his.

He tensed, and the exhilaration drained from him as his gaze locked with hers. His hand slid beneath her long hair, tilting her head to receive his kiss. There was no thought of objecting on Stephanie's part. Since the night in Paris, she'd longed for him to hold her. But she hadn't admitted how much she'd wanted it until now. He kissed her a second time, and his mouth was hungry and demanding. His lips moved persuasively over hers, hot and possessive. She was as hungry and eager for him. A slow fire burned through her and she melted against him. "Oh, Jonas," she whispered longingly.

He brushed his lips over hers a second time, then a third, as though he couldn't get enough of the taste of her. Stephanie opened her mouth to him, drugged by the sensations he aroused.

His mouth ravaged the scented hollow of her throat and began a slow meandering trail to her ear. He paused, took in a deep breath, and waited a moment longer before releasing her. "Forgive me." He brushed the wisps of hair from her temple. "That shouldn't have happened."

If he'd slapped her face, Stephanie wouldn't have been so insulted. She felt like a fool. She'd savored the feel of his arms, lost herself in the taste of his kiss and the rush of sensations that flooded her soul, and he was apologizing.

To add to her humiliation, her eyes filled with tears until his stiff, unyielding figure began to blur her vision.

"No apology is necessary," she murmured through the pain. "Just don't let it happen again."

Jonas hesitated as though he wanted to say something more, but then decided against it. Turning sharply, he stalked back to his desk.

Chapter Six

"Well?" Maureen was at Stephanie's desk early the following morning. "Don't keep me in suspense. What happened?"

"Nothing much." Stephanie kept her gaze lowered, doing her best not to reveal her emotions. She'd been depressed and out of sorts from the minute she left Jonas's office.

"Nothing much? What does that mean?"

"It means I don't want to talk about it."

"You had an argument?" Toni joined her friend. The two of them placed their hands on the edge of Stephanie's desk and leaned forward, as if what she had to say was a matter of national importance.

"I wish," Stephanie muttered, sighing heavily. "No, we didn't argue."

"But you don't want to talk about it?"

"Very perceptive, girls." She made busywork around her desk, inserting a pencil in the sharpener at the far edge of her desk. The grinding sound followed, but neither Toni nor Maureen budged.

"I think we need to talk to the others."

"You'll do no such thing," Stephanie insisted, her tone determined.

"Hey, come on, Steph, we're all in this together. We want to help. At least tell us what happened."

It was apparent that she wouldn't have a minute's peace until she confessed everything to her romance-loving friends. "Meet me at ten in the cafeteria," Stephanie told them. "I'll get it all over with at once, but only if you promise never to mention Jonas Lockwood's name to me again."

Toni and Maureen exchanged meaningful glances. "This doesn't sound good."

"It's my final offer." Replaying her humiliation was going to be bad enough; she didn't want it dragged out any more than necessary.

"All right, all right," Toni muttered. "We'll be there."

Stephanie's morning went smoothly. Her boss, George Potter, was on a two-day business trip to Seattle, but there was enough work to keep Stephanie occupied for another week if need be.

When she arrived in the cafeteria later that morning, she found the four women sitting at the table closest to the window, eagerly awaiting her arrival. A fifth cup of coffee was on the table in front of an empty chair.

"From that frown you're wearing, I'd say the meeting with Mr. Lockwood didn't go very well," Jan commented, barely giving Stephanie time to take a seat.

"There are no adequate words to describe it," Stephanie said by way of confirmation, reaching for the coffee. "I'm sorry to be such a major disappointment to you all, but anything that might have happened between me and Jonas Lockwood is off."

"Why?"

"What happened?"

"I could have sworn he was hooked."

"To be honest," Stephanie said, striving to be as forthright as possible, "I think Jonas may be attracted to me, but we're too different."

"That's what makes you so good together," Barbara countered.

"And I saw the way he looked at her," Jan inserted thoughtfully. "Now tell us what happened and let us figure out the next strategy."

Stephanie swallowed and shrugged. "If you must know, he kissed me."

"And you're complaining?"

"No, *he* was!"

"What?" All four looked at her as if she'd been working too much overtime.

"He kissed me, then immediately acted like he'd committed some terrible faux pas. The way he was looking at me, one would assume that I'd kissed him and he didn't like it in the least. He was angry and unreasonable, and worse, he insulted me with an apology."

"What did you say?"

"I told him never to let it happen again."

A chorus of moans and groans followed.

"You didn't!" Jan cried. "That was the worst thing you could have said."

"Well, it was his own fault," Stephanie flared, angry now. She'd been furious with him, and with herself. She'd liked it—in fact, she'd wished he had continued kissing her.

"Did you like it—the kiss I mean?" Toni looked at her hopefully.

Once again, Stephanie pretended to find her black coffee enthralling, and she centered her gaze on it. "Yes."

"How do you feel about Mr. Lockwood?"

"I . . . I don't know anymore."

"But if he'd asked you to dinner, you would have accepted the invitation?"

"Probably." Stephanie remembered the exhilaration in his eyes when he'd learned he'd gotten the permission of the French government to establish a branch of Lockwood Industries there. He worked so hard, and gave so much of himself to the business, that Stephanie experienced a sense of elation just watching him. She was happy for him and pleased to have played a small part in his triumph.

"But you can't give up."

"It was Jonas who did that," Stephanie said sharply.

"But he hasn't. Don't you see that?"

Stephanie glanced around the table, thinking her co-workers were playing some kind of joke on her. "I don't see it. Not at all."

"She hasn't read enough romances yet," Jan said, defending her friend. "She doesn't know."

"Mr. Lockwood is definitely attracted to you," Barbara claimed, with all the seriousness of a clinical psychologist. "Otherwise he wouldn't have reacted to the kiss the way you described."

"I'd hate to see how he'd react if he *didn't* like me," Stephanie said sarcastically. "I'm sorry, but it just isn't going to work. I'll even admit to being disappointed; he's not so bad once you get to know him. In fact, I might even have enjoyed falling in love with him." She admitted this at the expense of her own pride.

"It's hardly over yet," Maureen told her emphatically.

"Whose move is next?" Jan asked, looking around the table, seeking an answer from her peers.

"Mr. Lockwood's," Toni and Maureen said together, their heads nodding in unison.

"Definitely Lockwood's."

"Then I fear we've got a long wait coming," Stephanie informed them, finishing her coffee. "A very long wait."

"We'll see."

That same afternoon, Stephanie was typing at her desk when Jonas entered her office. He leaned heavily on his cane, waiting for her to notice him before he spoke.

Stephanie was aware of him the second he entered the room, but she finished the line she was typing before she turned her attention to the company president. Ignoring her pounding heart, she met his gaze squarely, refusing to give him the satisfaction of knowing the effect he had on her.

"Good afternoon, Mr. Lockwood," she said crisply. "Is there something I can do for you?"

"Miss Coulter." He paused and looked into Potter's office. "Is your boss available?"

Jonas had to know that he wasn't.

"Mr. Potter's in Seattle."

"Fine. Take a letter." He pulled up the chair and sat beside her desk.

Stephanie reached automatically for her steno pad, then paused. "Is Miss Westheimer ill again?"

"She was healthy the last time I looked."

"Then perhaps it would be better if she took your dictation." She raised her chin to a defiant angle, thinking as she did that her behavior would upset her friends. But she didn't care. She wouldn't let Jonas Lockwood boss her around even at the cost of a good job. Stephanie's hold on the pencil was so tight that it was a miracle it didn't snap in half.

"Address the letter to Miss Stephanie Coulter."

"Me?"

"Dear Ms. Coulter," he continued, ignoring her. "In thinking over the events of last evening, I am of the opinion that I owe you an apology."

As fast as her fingers could move the pencil, Stephanie transcribed his words. Not until her brain had assimilated the message did she pause. "I believe you already expressed your regret," she said stiffly. "You needn't have worried, I didn't take the kiss seriously."

"It was impulse."

"Right." She felt her anger flare. "And, as you say, best forgotten." But she couldn't forget it, even though she wanted to fling it to the farthest reaches of her mind. He'd held her and kissed her twice, and each time was engraved indelibly on her memory. Stephanie wondered if she'd ever be the same again.

Jonas scowled. "You're an attractive woman."

"I suppose I should thank you, but somehow that didn't sound like a compliment."

The frown thickened. "You could have any man you wanted."

Stephanie gave a self-deprecating laugh. "You seem to have an exaggerated opinion of my charms, Mr. Lockwood."

"I don't blame you for being offended that someone like me would kiss you."

"I wasn't offended." She was incensed that he'd even suggest such a thing. "If you want the truth, which you obviously do, I happened to find the whole experience rather pleasant."

"In Paris?"

"It was exactly what I wished for at the fountain, and you know it." Even as she said it, she knew how true it was. Since leaving his office the night before, she'd been in a blue funk, cranky and unreasonable and all because of Jonas. As much as she'd disliked him those few days she'd filled in for Bertha Westheimer, she admitted to liking him now. What she couldn't understand was why everything had changed. For days, sparks had flown every time they were in the same room. The sparks were still there, but they set off an entirely different kind of response now.

"My limp."

"What about your leg?" Deliberately, Stephanie set the pencil aside.

"Does it trouble you?"

She noticed the way his hand had tightened around the handle of his cane. His knuckles were stark white, and some of her outrage dissipated. "Of course not. Why should it?"

"Some women would be repelled by a cripple." He wouldn't look at her; his gaze rested on the filing cabinet on the opposite wall. "I want neither your sympathy nor your pity."

"That works out well, since you don't have either one." Her voice was crisp with impatience. She hated to believe that he had such a low opinion of her motives, but he gave her no choice but to think that.

"You could have your pick of any man in this company."

"Listen," she countered, her patience having long since evaporated. "It isn't like I've got a tribe of men seeking my company."

"You're attractive, bright and witty."

"Such high praise. I don't know how I should deal with it, especially when it comes from you, Mr. Lockwood."

Jonas was still studying the filing cabinet, ignoring her. "I can see that our little talk has helped clear away some misconceptions," he said.

"I certainly hope so."

"Have a good day, Ms. Coulter."

"You too, Mr. Lockwood."

Jonas had been gone five minutes before Stephanie fully accepted the fact that he'd actually been in her office. It took her another ten minutes to react. Her fingers were poised over the typewriter, ready to resume her task, when she realized she was shaking. She closed her eyes, and savored the warm feelings that washed over her in waves. Then she felt chilled; nerves skirted up and down her spine. Jan and the others had been right about Jonas. He was attracted to her, although he wore that stiff, businesslike facade like a heavy raincoat, not trusting her or the attraction they shared. He didn't have faith in her attraction to him, but she hoped that eventually he would realize her feelings were genuine.

Unable to contain her excitement, Stephanie reached for her phone and dialed Jan's extension.

"Personnel," Jan said when she answered.

"He was here."

"Who?"

"Guess," Stephanie said, laughing excitedly. "You were right. It was his move, and he made it."

"Mr. Lockwood?"

"Who else do you think I'm talking about?"

"I'll be right there."

Jan arrived a minute later, followed by Barbara, Toni and Maureen. "What did I tell you?" Jan said excitedly, slapping Barbara's open hand with her own.

"There isn't time for you to read more romances," Toni murmured, looking worried.

"The only thing she can do now is follow her instincts," Maureen said brightly. "He's interested. She's interested. Everything will follow its natural course."

"What do you mean 'natural course'?" Stephanie asked, concerned. This was beginning to sound a lot like kidney stones.

"Marriage." They said the word in unison, and looked at her as though her elevator didn't go all the way to the top floor. "It's what we're all after."

"Marriage?" Stephanie repeated slowly. Everything was happening too fast for her to react.

"But you like him," Toni challenged.

"Hey, wait a minute, you guys. Sure I like Jonas Lockwood, but liking is a long way from marriage."

"You're perfect together." Maureen was incredulous that Stephanie could question her fate. The four romance-lovers had everything arranged, and her resistance wasn't appreciated.

"Perfect together? Jonas and me?" Stephanie frowned. The two of them did more arguing than anything. They were only beginning to come to an understanding.

"You have to plan your strategy carefully."

"My strategy?"

"Right." Barbara nodded.

"You'll need to make him believe that love and marriage are all his idea."

"Don't you think we could start by holding hands?"

"Very funny," Jan said, placing her hand on her hip.

"I feel it's more important to let this relationship fall into its own time frame." Stephanie looked up at the four who were standing around her desk, arms crossed, staring disapprovingly down at her. "That is, if there's going to *be* a relationship."

Together they all shook their heads. "Wrong."

"Okay, what are you planning next?" Jan asked.

"Me?" Stephanie held her hand to her breast. "I'm not planning anything. Should I be?"

"Of course; Mr. Lockwood made his move, now it's your turn."

This romance business sounded a lot like playing chess. "I . . . hadn't given it any thought."

"Well, don't worry, we'll figure out something. Are you doing anything after work?"

"Depositing my check, and picking up the bookcase I've had on layaway."

"Well, for heaven's sake, what's more important?" Jan gave her an incredulous look.

"You want the truth?" Stephanie glanced around at her friends. It didn't matter if she was with them or not; they were going to plot her life to their own satisfaction. "I'm going with the bookcase. If you four come up with something brilliant, phone me."

Several pieces of polished wood lay across Stephanie's carpet, along with a bowl full of screws. The screwdriver was clenched between her teeth as she struggled with the instructions. The phone rang, and she absently reached for it, forgetting about the screwdriver.

"Hebbloo."

"Stephanie?"

"Jonas?" Her heartbeat instantly quickened as she grabbed the screwdriver from between her lips. For one crazy second, she actually wanted to tell him he couldn't contact her—it was her move!

"I hope this isn't a bad time."

"No...no, of course it isn't. I wasn't doing anything." She stared at the disembodied pieces of the bookcase scattered across her carpet, and added, "Important."

"I know it's short notice, but I was wondering if you were free to join me for dinner."

"Dinner?" Stephanie knew she sounded amazingly like an echo. Again she toyed with the idea of contacting Jan before she agreed to do anything with Jonas, but just as quickly rejected that thought. Her co-workers were making her paranoid.

"If you have company or..."

"No, I'm alone." She picked up the instructions for assembling the bookcase and sighed. "Jonas, do you speak Danish?"

"Pardon?"

"How about Swedish?"

"No. Why?"

At this point, she was so frustrated she wanted to cry. "It's not important."

"About dinner?"

"Yes, I'd love to go." Never mind that she had a roast in the oven with small potatoes and fresh peas in the sink ready to be boiled.

"I'll pick you up in a few minutes then."

"Great." Stephanie glanced down at her faded Levi's, ten-year-old sweatshirt, and purple Reeboks, and groaned. She picked up the receiver to phone Jan, decided she didn't have enough time, and hurried into her room. The sweatshirt came off first and was flung to the farthest corner of her small bedroom. She found a soft pink silk blouse hanging in her closet and quickly inserted her arms. Her fingers shook as she rushed to work the small pearl buttons.

She had the jeans down around her thighs when the doorbell chimed. Stephanie closed her eyes and prayed that it wasn't Jonas. It couldn't be! He'd only phoned a couple of minutes ago. She jumped, hauling her jeans back up to her waist, and ran to the door, yanking it open.

"Listen, I'm sorry if I sound rude, but I don't have the time to buy anything right now—" Stephanie stopped abruptly, wishing the earth would open up and swallow her. Her breath caught in her throat and she closed her eyes momentarily. "Hello, Jonas."

"Did you know your pants are unzipped?"

She whirled around, sucked in her stomach and pulled up the zipper. "I didn't expect you so soon."

"Obviously. I called from a pay phone across the street."

"Please come in. I'll only be a few minutes." If he so much as snickered, Stephanie swore, she'd find a way to take revenge. Some form of justice fitting the crime, like a pot roast dumped over his head.

Jonas glanced around at the pieces of wood strewn across her carpet. "You're building something?"

"A bookcase." She'd hoped to have that cleaned up before he arrived, but that had been her second concern. She'd wanted to be dressed first. A soft cough that sounded suspiciously like a smothered laugh came from Jonas.

"Did you say something?" Her hands knotted at her side, and she eyed the oven where the pot roast was cooking.

"I don't believe I've ever seen you flustered before." His look was amused, and his voice soft and gruff at the same time. "Not Stephanie Coulter, the woman who defies and challenges me at every turn."

"Try answering the door with your underwear showing. It has a humbling effect."

Jonas chuckled, and the sound had a musical quality to it. Despite her embarrassment, Stephanie laughed with him, feeling completely at ease with him for the first time since Paris. "I'll only be a few minutes."

"Take your time."

She was halfway to her bedroom when she stopped, realizing that she'd forgotten her manners in her eagerness to escape. "Would you like something to drink while you wait?"

"No, thanks." He picked up the assembly instructions for the bookcase, which were on the end table by the phone. "Danish?" he asked, cocking both brows.

"I guess. It may be Swedish or Greek. I can't tell."

His gaze scanned the pieces on the floor. "Would you like a little help?"

"I'd like a lot of help." A wry smile twisted her mouth. She'd spent the better part of two hours attempting to make sense of the diagram and the foreign instructions.

"Do I detect a note of resignation in your voice, Ms. Coulter?"

"That's not resignation, it's out-and-out frustration, disillusionment, and more than a touch of anger."

"I'll see what I can do."

Stephanie started to leave, but when she saw Jonas take off his suit jacket and reach for one long piece of shelving to join it to another, she paused. "That won't work." Soon she was kneeling on the floor opposite Jonas. She began to feel like a nurse assisting a brain surgeon, handing Jonas one part after another. In frustration, he paused to study the diagram, turning it upside down and around, just as she had done, but still couldn't figure out which pieces linked.

"Wait," Jonas said, shaking his head. "We've been doing this all wrong."

Stephanie groaned, and mumbled under her breath. "The man's a genius."

"If I was such a whiz, these bookcases would have books in them by now," Jonas grumbled, his brow knit in a thoughtful frown. "Give me the screwdriver, would you?"

"Sure." Stephanie, who was kneeling close to his side, handed it to him.

Jonas turned to thank her. Their eyes met, and they stared at each other for an endless moment. Stephanie blinked and looked away first. Never before had she been so aware of Jonas as a man. He looked different than any time she'd seen him in the office. Younger. Less worried. Almost boyishly handsome. He made no move to touch her, yet Stephanie felt a myriad of sensations shoot through her as though he had. He was so close she could smell the spicy scent of his after-shave and feel the warmth of his hard, lean body as it seeped into her, chasing away the chill of her insecurities. She could feel his breath against her hair, and she welcomed it, swaying toward him.

Stephanie didn't know who moved first. It didn't matter. Before she was aware of anything, they were on their knees with their arms wrapped around each other. Stephanie closed her eyes and let the warm sensation of his touch thread through her limbs. His hands gripped her upper arms as he moved his mouth to hers. His kiss was tentative, exploring, as though he expected her to stop him. Stephanie couldn't; she'd been wanting him to hold and kiss her for days. His lips were open, warm, suckling as they covered her own. The tip of his tongue traced her lips, and she eagerly opened her mouth to his exploration.

Stephanie's fingers moved from his hard chest and she slid her arms up and around the thick column of his neck, flattening her torso to his. His hands were splayed across her back, drawing her nearer as his tongue slipped between her silken lips and his kiss grew greedy, hungry, and demanding. Her breasts peaked, yearning for his hands.

When his fingers moved to cup her breast, Stephanie's body throbbed with wild sensations, and a small moan of satisfaction slid up her throat. His thumb stroked the crest, and Stephanie felt her nipple harden in immediate response.

Her hands reveled in the feel of the hard muscles of his shoulder and the softness of the thick hair at the base of his neck. A delicious languor spread through her.

Jonas buried his face in the hollow of her throat and shuddered. "Stephanie?"

"Humm." She felt warm and wonderful.

"I don't know what it is, but something smells like it's burning."

Stephanie's eyes flew open. She let out a small cry of alarm and jumped to her feet.

Chapter Seven

Oh, Jonas, the roast." She grabbed two pot holders and pulled open the oven to retrieve the pot roast. Black smoke filled the small kitchen, and Stephanie waved her hand to clear the air. "So much for that," she said, heaving an exasperated sigh.

"What is it?" Jonas joined her, examining the charred piece of meat.

"What does it look like?" she said hotly, then stared at the crisp roast and slowly shook her head. "If you have any kindness left in your heart, you won't answer that."

Chuckling, Jonas slipped his arm around her shoulders. "There are worse disasters."

"I imagine you're referring to an unassembled bookcase with instructions in a foreign language."

Amusement glinted in his blue eyes at the belligerent way her mouth thinned. Stephanie couldn't help pouting. She was furious with herself for ruining a perfectly good piece of meat, and what was even worse was to have to face this disgrace in front of Jonas.

"Come on," he prompted. "There's a fabulous Chinese restaurant near here. The kitchen can air out while we're gone, and when we get back, I'll finish putting that bookcase together."

"All right," she agreed, and her mouth curved into a weak smile. Jonas was right. The best thing she could do was to draw his attention away from her lack of culinary skill. If he continued to see her, she'd know for certain that it wasn't her talent in the kitchen that had attracted him.

It was not until Stephanie had buckled the seat belt in Jonas's Mercedes that she realized she was still wearing her faded, washed-out jeans and her tennis shoes. "This Chinese restaurant isn't fancy, is it?" She placed her hand over the knee that showed white through the threadbare blue jeans.

Jonas's gaze followed hers. "Poor Stephanie." He chuckled. "You're having quite a night, aren't you?"

She folded her hands in her lap and crossed her legs. "It's an average night." Better than most. Worse than some. It wasn't every day that Jonas Lockwood held her in his arms and kissed her until her world spun out of its orbit. Just thinking about the way he'd held her produced a warm glow inside her until she was certain she must radiate with it.

"You do enjoy Chinese food?"

"Oh, yes."

"By the way, do you often wear purple tennis shoes?"

Startled, Stephanie glanced down at her feet and experienced another minor twinge of regret. "I bought them on sale—they were half-price."

Jonas chuckled. "I think it was the color."

"I usually only wear them around the apartment," she said, only a little offended. "They work fine for *The Twenty-Minute Workout*."

"The what?"

"*The Twenty-Minute Workout*? It's on every morning at six. Don't you ever watch it?" She wasn't sure the neighbor in the apartment below appreciated her jumping around the living room at such an ungodly hour, but Mrs. Humphrey had never complained.

"I take it you're referring to a televised exercise program."

"Yes. Have you heard of it?"

"No, I prefer my club."

"Oh, the joys of being rich." She said it with a sigh of feigned envy.

"Are you going to complain about your wages?"

"Would it do any good?"

"No."

"That's what I thought." Her gaze slid to him, and again she marveled at the man at her side. The top buttons of his white business shirt were unfastened, exposing bronze skin and dark curly hair. The long sleeves were rolled up, revealing the eagerness with which he'd helped her with the bookcase. He stopped at a red light, and seemed to feel her eyes on him. His gaze met hers, and Stephanie noted the fine lines that feathered out from the corners of his eyes. The grooves at the side of his mouth, which she had so often thought of as harsh, softened now as he smiled. Jonas Lockwood was a different man when he grinned. It transformed his entire face.

Stephanie was astonished how much his smile could affect her. Her heart stopped, then started up again, pounding the blood hotly through her veins. If given the least bit of encouragement, Stephanie would have impulsively eliminated the small space that separated them and pressed her mouth to his, revealing with a kiss how much being with him had stirred her heart.

She reluctantly dragged her gaze from his and glanced down at her hands folded neatly in her lap. In that instant, as brief as it was, Stephanie recognized the truth. She was falling in love with Jonas Lockwood, and she was falling hard. Up to this point in their nonrelationship, she had considered him an intriguing challenge. Jan, Maureen and the others had piqued her interest in their domineering, arrogant employer. The trip to Paris, and their time at the fountain in the park had added to her curiosity. She'd glimpsed the man buried deep inside the gruff exterior, and had been enthralled. Now she was caught, hook, line and sinker.

Long after they'd returned from dinner and the finished bookcase stood in the corner of her living room, Stephanie recalled the look they'd exchanged in the car on the way to the restaurant. Briefly she wondered if Jonas had recognized it for what it was. Certainly the evening had been altered because of that glance. Before that instant in the car they had been teasing each other and joking, but from the moment they entered the restaurant, they had immersed themselves in serious conversation. Jonas wanted to know everything about her. And Stephanie talked for hours. She told him about growing up in Colville, and what living in the country had meant to a gawky, young girl. When he asked how she happened to move to Minneapolis, Stephanie explained that her godparents lived nearby, and had encouraged her to move into the area. There were other relatives close by as well, and there were precious few secretarial positions in the eastern part of Washington State.

It wasn't until their plates were cleared away and the waiter delivered two fortune cookies that Stephanie realized that while she'd been telling him her life story, Jonas had revealed little about himself. She felt guilty about dominating the conversation, but when she mentioned it, Jonas brushed her concern aside, telling her there was plenty of time for her to get to know him better. For hours afterward, Stephanie was on a natural high, exhilarated and happy. She enjoyed talking to Jonas, and for the first time since Paris, they were at ease with each other.

When Stephanie arrived at work the following morning, there was a message on her desk from Jan. The note asked Stephanie to join her and the others in the cafeteria on their coffee break. All morning, Stephanie toyed with the idea of telling her friends about the evening she'd spent with Jonas, but finally decided against it. The night had been so special that she wanted to wrap the feelings she'd experienced with Jonas around herself and keep them private.

At midmorning, she found the four gathered around the same table by the window that they'd occupied earlier in the week. Again, her coffee was waiting for her.

"Morning."

"You're late," Jan scolded, glancing at her watch. "We've got a lot of ground to cover."

"We do?" Stephanie glanced around the table at her friends and wondered if the Geneva peace talks held more somber, serious faces.

"It's your move with Mr. Lockwood," Maureen explained. "And we've been up half the night discussing the best way for you to approach him."

"I see." Stephanie took a sip of her coffee to hide an amused grin.

"Subtlety is the key," Barbara inserted. "It's imperative that he doesn't know that you've planned this next *chance* meeting."

"Would it be so wrong to let him know I'm interested?" Stephanie let her gaze fall to the table so that her friends couldn't read her expression.

"That comes later," Toni told her. "This next step is the all-important one."

"I see." Stephanie didn't, but she doubted that her lack of understanding concerned her friends. "So what's the next move?"

"That's the problem—we can't decide," Jan explained. "We seem to be at a standstill."

"It's a toss-up between four different ideas."

One from each romantic, Stephanie reasoned.

"I thought you could wait until Old Stone Face has left her guard post for the day, and then make up an excuse to go to his office—any excuse would do—for that matter, I could give you one," Jan said eagerly. "You're on his turf, where he's most comfortable. Of course, you'll need to find a way to get close to him. You know, bend over the desk so your heads meet and your fingers accidently brush against his. From there, everything will work out great."

"But I don't like that idea," Maureen muttered, slowly shaking her head. "Besides, Mr. Lockwood's too intelligent not to see through that ploy."

"George Potter is always taking one thing or another up to Jonas's office. I could volunteer to do it for him; I'm sure he wouldn't mind," Stephanie said, defending Jan's idea.

"Yes, but from everything I've read, it'd be better if we forced his hand."

"Force his hand? What do you mean?" Stephanie glanced at Maureen.

"Let him see you with another man."

"But that's already happened, with disastrous results," Jan argued. "Besides, where are we going to come up with another man?"

"My husband's brother is available."

"Ladies, please," Stephanie cried, raising both hands to squelch that plan. "I've got to agree with any scheme you come up with, and that one is most definitely a *no*."

"Sympathy always works," Barbara said thoughtfully. "I've read lots of romances where the turning point in the relationship comes when either the hero or the heroine becomes ill or is seriously hurt."

For a moment, Stephanie actually believed her friends were about to suggest she came down with the mumps or chicken pox just so she could garner Jonas's sympathy.

"I've got a cousin who works for an orthopedic surgeon. He could put a cast on Stephanie so Mr. Lockwood would think she had a broken leg." Again Barbara glanced around the table, wanting the others' reactions.

In her mind, Stephanie could see herself hobbling to and from work for weeks in a plaster cast up to her hip while she carried out this ridiculous charade. She couldn't very well arrive the next day without the cast and announce to everyone that a miracle had occurred.

"No go." She nixed that plan before the four could endorse it and she ended up in a body cast without ever knowing how it happened. "What's wrong with me inviting him over to my apartment for dinner?"

"It's so obvious," Barbara groaned.

"And the rest of your ideas aren't?"

"Now something like that just might work," Jan said thoughtfully, chewing on the end of her index finger. "It's not brilliant, but it has possibilities."

"There's only one problem," Stephanie informed her friends, remembering the charred pot roast from the night before. "I'm not much of a cook."

"That's not a problem. You could hire a chef to come in, and Mr. Lockwood need never know."

"Isn't that a bit expensive?" Stephanie could visualize the balance in her checkbook rapidly reaching the point of no return.

"It's worth a try." Barbara rapidly discounted Stephanie's concern.

"What was your idea, Toni?" Everyone had revealed their schemes except the small brunette.

She shrugged. "Nothing great—I thought you might 'accidentally on purpose' meet Mr. Lockwood by the elevator sometime. You could strike up a casual conversation and let matters follow their natural course."

"But Steph could end up spending the entire workday hanging around the elevator," Barbara said, her voice raised at what she considered an unreasonable plan.

"Not only that," Jan added, "but who's to say that the elevator will be empty? She'd look too obvious if there were other people aboard."

Stephanie's gaze flew from one intent face to the other. "I like that scheme best."

"What?" Three pairs of shocked eyes shot to Stephanie.

"Well, for heaven's sake! With the rest of your ideas, I'm either going to have to subject myself to Bertha Westheimer's scrutiny, date Barbara's brother-in-law, sheath my body in plaster or deplete my checking account to hire a chef to cook for me. Toni's idea is the only one that makes any sense."

"But you suggested inviting him to dinner," Jan informed her.

Maureen folded her hands on the table top and studied Stephanie through narrowed eyes. "You know, it suddenly dawned on me that you're not fighting us anymore, Steph."

"No," she said and reached for her coffee, curving her fingers around the cup. She took a drink and when she set it back down, she noted that the four had become silent.

"In fact, if you've noticed, she's even adding her own ideas." Jan's look was approving.

"Could it be that you've come to have some feelings for Mr. Lockwood?" Barbara asked.

"It could be that I find the man a challenge."

"It's more than that," Toni said quietly. "I noticed when you first joined us this morning that there was something different about you."

It shows, Stephanie mused, a bit irritated.

"What do you feel for Mr. Lockwood?"

"I'm not completely sure yet," Stephanie admitted honestly. "He makes me so angry I could shake him."

"But..."

"But then, at other times, he looks at me and we share a smile and I want to melt on the inside." She knew her eyes must have revealed her feelings, because the others grew even quieter.

"Could you see yourself married to him?"

Stephanie didn't need to think twice about that. "Yes." They'd argue, and disagree, and challenge each other—that was a given—but the loving between them would be exquisite.

The unexpected shout of joy that followed her announcement nearly knocked Stephanie out of her chair. "Good grief, be quiet," she cried, her hand over her heart. "We're a long way from the altar."

"Not nearly as far as you think, honey," Barbara said with a wide, knowing grin. "Not nearly as far as you think."

Stephanie left the cafeteria a couple of minutes later. In spite of everything, she had to struggle not to laugh. Her four self-proclaimed romantic friends seemed to believe that a couple of dinners—one of which they knew nothing about—and a few stolen kisses in the moonlight constituted marriage.

When she arrived at her desk, Stephanie placed her purse in the bottom drawer, sat down and pulled out some paper, preparing to type a letter. She paused, her hands poised over the keyboard, trying to analyze her feelings for Jonas. The page in front of her blurred as she remembered his kisses. From the look about him, he was as surprised as she was. The minute they'd met, Stephanie had disliked the man. He was so dictatorial and high-handed that he infuriated her. He enjoyed baiting her and challenging her. In some ways, Jonas Lockwood was the most difficult man she'd ever known. But at the same time, Stephanie suspected that the rewards of his love would be beyond any worldly treasure she hoped to accumulate.

At five that evening, Stephanie cleared off the top of her desk, preparing to head home to her apartment. It was so late by the time Jonas finished assembling the bookcase that she hadn't had the energy to fill it with the books that were propped against her bedroom wall. She'd learned as the evening progressed that Jonas was an avid reader, and they'd had a lively discussion on their favorite authors. When he'd left her apartment, it had been close to midnight. She'd thanked him for dinner and his help with the bookcase, and had been mildly disappointed that he hadn't kissed her good night. Nor did he arrange for another meeting. At the time, Stephanie hadn't given the matter a second thought. Now she wondered how long it would be before she saw Jonas again. She was a bit discouraged not to have heard from him before now. All day, she'd been half expecting him to pop in unannounced and dictate another letter to her. The entire afternoon felt strangely incomplete, and she realized that she'd been wanting to hear from him since the minute she arrived that morning.

On her way to the elevator, Stephanie spotted Jonas talking to Donald Black, head of the accounting department. Her pulse quickened at the virile sight Jonas presented. He was an attractive figure, tall and broad-shouldered, and—she freely admitted it—he was a handsome devil. Her heart swelled at the sight of him, and when his gaze happened to catch hers, Stephanie smiled warmly, revealing all the pleasure she felt at seeing him again.

Jonas didn't respond. If anything, he almost looked right through her, as if she were nothing more than a piece of furniture. If any emotion showed on his taut features, it was regret. Stephanie swallowed, feeling as if she had a pine cone lodged in her throat.

When he did happen to glance in her direction, Stephanie read the demand in his eyes. What happened outside the office was between them, but inside Lockwood Industries she was nothing more than a secretary, and she'd do well to remember that.

Humiliated and insulted, Stephanie stiffened and looked past him as though he were a stranger, pretending she had neither the time nor the energy to play his infantile games. She thrust her shoulders back in a display of anger and pride, and held them so stiffly that her shoulder blades ached within seconds.

From the minute Jonas had left her the night before, Stephanie had been happy and content. Now her spirits plummeted to the bottom floor at breakneck speed and landed with a sickening thud. She turned her gaze to the front of the elevator and refused to look at him another moment.

She heard the two men walking behind her, but Stephanie ignored them both.

"Good evening, Miss Coulter," Jonas said in passing.

"Good evening, sir," she responded tightly, in a professional crisp tone.

The elevator arrived, and without another word, Stephanie joined the others in the five o'clock rush. She rode the elevator to the street level, and five minutes later caught Metro bus #17 that dropped her off a block from her apartment.

Affronted by his attitude, chagrined at how much she had read into the simple evening they'd shared, and disgruntled that she'd allowed Jan and friends to talk her into believing Jonas Lockwood had a heart, Stephanie quickly changed clothes and decided to weed her miniature herb garden.

She hadn't been home more than thirty minutes when the doorbell chimed. Glaring at her front door, she continued pulling up the weeds in the small redwood planters, then stared down at her garden gloves and realized she'd uprooted more basil than anything else.

She didn't need to answer the door to know it was Jonas who stood on the other side. When the doorbell rang sharply a second time, Stephanie impatiently set the trowel aside and stood up.

She muttered under her breath as she marched across the living room floor, and swore that if he commented on her purple tennis shoes one more time she would slam the door in his face. She jerked off a dirt-covered glove and pulled open the door.

"Hello, Stephanie."

"Mr. Lockwood," she responded tautly. "What an unpleasant surprise."

"May I come in?"

"No." She avoided his eyes. It took all her willpower not to close the door and be done with him. But she'd decided to play this little charade out. She might not come from a rich, powerful family like Jonas's, but she didn't lack pride. "As you can see, I'm busy," she finished.

"This will only take a minute."

"I'm surprised you're lowering yourself to come here," she added waspishly. "Your message this afternoon came through crystal-clear."

"I'd like to explain that." Disregarding her unfriendly welcome and her unwillingness to allow him into her apartment, Jonas stalked past her and into the living room.

"It seems I have no say in the matter. All right, since you're so keen to explain yourself, do so and then kindly leave."

"I honestly would like to explain—"

"Go ahead," she cried. "But let me assure you, it isn't necessary."

Jonas leaned heavily on his cane as he walked to the center of the room. Stephanie stubbornly remained at the front door. She'd closed it, but stood ready to yank it open the minute he finished.

He turned to face her, and placed both hands on the curve of the polished oak cane, using it for support.

"I realize the name Coulter may not cause a banker's heart to flutter, but it's a good name. My father's proud of it, and so am I."

"Stephanie, you misunderstood my intentions."

"I sincerely doubt that." Her voice trembled with the strength of her emotion. "I understood you perfectly."

His eyes were blue and probing as they swept her tightly controlled features. She wondered if a splattering of mud was smeared across her cheek, but wouldn't give him the satisfaction of running her fingers over her face to find out. No doubt he'd view it as a sign of weakness. She *was* weak, she realized, but only when he held her and kissed her, and she wouldn't allow that now.

"It wouldn't matter to me if your name was Getty, or Rockefeller, or Hughes for that matter. Don't you understand that?"

"Obviously not," she returned stiffly. "You were putting me in my place, and you did a good job of it, I might add. I'm a lowly, brainless secretary and you're the big, mighty boss, and I shouldn't confuse the two. Since I'm not the mature woman you prefer, I would do well to bow low whenever your shadow passes near me. Isn't that what you meant to say?"

"No. Damn it, I should have known you'd be unreasonable."

"Me? Unreasonable? That's a laugh. I've worked for Mr. Potter for nearly two years, and we've never exchanged a cross word. Two seconds in your company and I'm so angry I can hardly think."

"Would you stop with this lowly secretary bit? I wouldn't care if you were the first vice president," he shouted. "Anything that's between you and me has to stay out of the office!"

"Of course it must," she simpered. "It would do your reputation considerable harm if anyone knew you'd lowered yourself to actually date an employee."

"It's not me I'm thinking about."

"You could have fooled me."

"Stephanie, if you'd get off your high horse a minute, you'd see that it's good business. Hell, I probably shouldn't be seeing you now; I'm supposed to be at a meeting."

She jerked open the door. "Don't let me stop you." Stephanie recognized the flash of anger in his eyes and experienced a small sense of triumph.

He ran a hand over his face, wiping his expression clean as he fought for control of his considerable temper. "Can't you understand that I'm doing this for your own protection?"

"Forgive me for being dense, but quite frankly, I don't."

He continued as though she hadn't spoken. "Some no-good busybody is going to drag your name through the mud the minute they learn we're seeing each other. The next thing either of us knows, you'll be the subject of jealous, malicious gossip. You won't be able to walk into a room without people whispering your name."

Stephanie swallowed convulsively. "I hadn't thought of... that." Her friends were supportive, but they were only a small fraction of the personnel employed by Lockwood Industries.

"A thousand times, I told myself that seeing you would only lead to trouble." A dark, brooding look clouded his eyes. "Even now, I'm not convinced it's right for either of us."

Stephanie had to swallow down the words to argue with him. It felt incredibly right to be with Jonas.

"If you're seeking my apology for what happened earlier," he said in a gruff, low-pitched voice, "then you have it. It has never been my intention to offend you."

"I owe you an apology as well." With her hands clasped in front of her, Stephanie took a step toward him. "You're right about the office, Jonas, only I was too much of an idiot to see it."

He smiled one of those rare, rich smiles of his, a smile that Stephanie was convinced could melt stone. "I'm pleased we cleared away this misunderstanding," he said, and glanced at his watch, frowning. "Now I really must be going."

"Thank you for coming." Knowing that he'd found it important to explain meant a great deal to her.

He walked to the door, then suddenly turned to her. "Do you sail?"

"Sure." She'd never been on a sailboat in her life. "At least, I think I can, given the chance."

"How about this weekend?"

"I'd like that very much."

"I'll call you later," he said on his way out the door. Then he muttered something about her not making bankers' hearts flutter, but doing a hell of a good job of his own.

Stephanie closed the door after him and leaned against it, grinning with a smile that beamed all the way from her heart.

Chapter Eight

A stiff breeze billowed the huge spinnaker, and the thirty-foot sailboat heeled sharply, shaving the waterline with a razor-sharp cut. Stephanie threw back her head and laughed merrily into the wind. The pins holding her hair had long ago been discarded, and her blond tresses now unfurled behind her like a flag, waving in the crisp air. "Oh Jonas, I love this."

His answering smile was warm. "Somehow I knew you'd be a natural on the water."

"This is marvelous." She crossed her arms over her breasts as though to hug the sense of exhilaration she felt.

"You've never sailed before?"

"Never." She noted the way he steered the boat from the helm, his movements confident, sure. "Can I do that?"

"If you'd like."

Stephanie joined him and sat down at his side. "Okay, tell me what to do."

"Just head her into the wind."

"Okay." She placed both hands on the long narrow handle that controlled the rudder and watched as the boat turned sharply. Almost immediately the sails went slack, but one guiding touch from Jonas and they filled with wind again.

"Hey, this isn't as easy as it looks," Stephanie complained, though not strenuously. The day was marvelous. There wasn't any other way to describe it, but the weather had little to do with Stephanie's evaluation of this particular Saturday.

Jonas had arrived at her apartment early that morning, bringing freshly squeezed orange juice, croissants still warm from the oven, and two large cups of steaming coffee. Stephanie had always been a morning person, and Jonas apparently was as well.

She had prepared her own surprise by packing them a picnic lunch. Included in her basket were two small loaves of French bread, a bottle of white wine, a variety of cheeses and some fresh strawberries that had cost her more than she cared to think about. But one look at the plump, juicy fruit and Stephanie couldn't resist them.

The journey into Duluth was pleasant, as Jonas spoke of his family and their home on Lake Superior. His mother lived there now, and Stephanie would be meeting her later that afternoon.

"You're quiet all of a sudden," Jonas mentioned as he reached over to correct her steering once again. "Is anything troubling you?"

"How could anything possibly be wrong on a glorious day like this one?"

"You were frowning."

"I was?" Stephanie glanced out over the choppy water. There wasn't another boat in sight. It was as though she and Jonas alone faced the mighty power of this astonishing lake. "I was thinking about meeting your mother. I guess I'm nervous."

"Why should you be?"

"Jonas, look at me. I could be confused with a fugitive from justice in these old jeans; I only wish you'd said something earlier so I could have brought a change of clothes along."

"Mother won't care."

Perhaps not, Stephanie mused, but *she* certainly did. If she was going to come face-to-face with Jonas's mother, Stephanie would have preferred to do it when she looked her best. Not now, with her hair in tangles and knots from the wind and her face free of makeup and a pinkish-red from the day in the sun. On the other hand, Stephanie's musings continued, Mrs. Lockwood would see her at her worst and be pleasantly surprised if she met her later. Her lazy smile grew and grew, and she glanced at Jonas.

His look was thoughtful. "Stephanie, I don't want you to fret about meeting my family."

"She must be a marvelous woman."

"As a matter of fact she is, but you sound as if you know her, and that isn't possible."

Stephanie's gaze momentarily scanned the swirling green water in an effort to avoid meeting his intense gaze. "You're right, I could pass her on the street and not know who she is, but she's a special person." The woman who bore and raised Jonas would have to be.

Jonas placed his arm around her shoulder, and Stephanie leaned her head back against the solid cushion of his chest. Gently, he kissed the top of her head.

Stephanie turned so that her lips touched his throat where his shirt opened. His skin was warm, and she both felt and heard his answering sigh. His large hand was splayed against the back of her head, and he directed her mouth to his. Stephanie didn't need any more encouragement, and their mouths met in a gentle brushing of lips. She moved away from the helm and slipped her arms around his neck. He kissed her again, longer this time, much longer, but still he was infinitely gentle, as though he feared hurting her. Jonas released her when the sails began to flap in the wind, but he did it with such reluctance that Stephanie's heart sang.

"Are you hungry?" she asked, more for something to do than from any desire for lunch.

"Yes," Jonas admitted hoarsely, but when she went toward the wicker picnic basket, Jonas's hand caught hers, delaying her.

Stephanie raised questioning eyes to his. "Jonas?"

In a heartbeat, he gently pulled her back to him, his hand slipping around her waist. "It isn't food that tempts me." He kissed her again, his mouth moving on hers with an urgency as old as mankind itself. Stephanie threaded her fingers through his hair and held his head fast as his tongue brushed against hers until she was so weak that she slumped against him.

"Jonas," she breathed as his hand slid up the front of her shirt to cup her breasts. They swelled in his hands, throbbing, aching, begging for his touch. With limitless patience, he raised her blouse, freeing her breasts of the confining lace. Her breath caught in her throat as his lips sought her nipple. She could feel the heat of his mouth, closing snugly around the pink crest of her breast. He tasted it and kissed it until Stephanie tossed back her head to better capture the wild sensation that erupted within her. When he'd finished with one breast, he moved to the other, gently rolling the beaded nipple with his tongue. Had Stephanie had the power to draw in a breath, she would have gasped and cried out at the pleasure he was giving her. Her fingers dug deeper into his hair, and moisture filled her eyes. Nothing she had ever experienced with a man had been this beautiful. Nothing had ever been so intimate. She felt as if her breasts were melting like spun sugar against his tongue. A sound must have slipped from her throat, because Jonas paused and slowly raised his head.

Almost immediately he noticed the tears brimming in her eyes. "Did I hurt you?"

She quickly shook her head. "No, oh no, you couldn't."

He brought her down so that they were sitting side by side. His arms came around her, and he fused his mouth to hers. Again and again he kissed her, tasting, nipping at her lower lip until Stephanie thought she would go mad with wanting him. Her hand crept up his hard chest and closed around the folds of his collar. The kiss was long and thorough. This day with Jonas was the sweetest she had ever known.

With his arms wrapped securely around her shoulders, Stephanie swayed with the gentle rocking of the boat, lulled by the peace that surrounded them. Jonas had somehow lowered the sails without her even knowing it. He continued to hold her, staring out over the rolling water. Not for the first time, Stephanie noted that his eyes were incredibly blue. As though sensing her scrutiny, Jonas gazed down at her. For a long moment they stared at each other, lost in the world that had been created just for them and for this moment.

Some time later, Jonas reached for the picnic basket. He brought out a plump red strawberry, plucked the stem from the top of the red fruit, and fed it to Stephanie. She bit into the pulp, and a thin line of juice ran down her chin. As she moved to wipe it away, Jonas's hand stopped hers. He bent his index finger, and with his knuckle rubbed the red juice aside. Then, very slowly, as though he couldn't resist, he lowered his mouth to hers. Their lips met and clung. His grip tightened as his tongue sought and found hers. When he lifted his mouth from hers, he smiled gently. The moisture pooled in her eyes, and a tear slipped from the corner of her eye and rolled down her cheek.

A puzzled frown knit Jonas's brow. "You're crying."

"I know."

"I hurt you?"

"No."

"Then why?"

She turned her head into his shoulder, convinced he would laugh once he knew.

"Stephanie?"

"It was so beautiful. I always cry when I'm this happy." Feeling foolish, she rubbed her hands against her eyes. "It's a family curse. My mother weeps every Christmas."

Jonas reached for the wine, opened it, and poured them each a glass.

"Alcohol won't help," she said, sniffling, but she didn't refuse the glass Jonas offered her.

"Are there any other family curses I should know about?"

"I have a bit of a temper."

Jonas chuckled. "I've encountered that."

Laughing lightly, Stephanie straightened and took her first sip of wine. It felt cool and tasted sweet, reminding her that she was hungry. "Some bread?" she asked, looking at him.

Jonas leaned forward to reach for it, and as he did, a look of pain shot across his face, widening his eyes. He sat back quickly.

"Jonas?" Concerned, Stephanie turned to him. "What is it?"

"It'll pass in a moment."

"What will pass?"

"The pain," he gritted, stroking the length of his thigh in an effort to ease the agony. He closed his eyes and turned away from her.

Stephanie bent in front of him, nearly frantic. "Tell me what I can do."

"Nothing," he said through clenched teeth. "Go away."

"No," she shouted. "I won't leave you alone." Because she didn't know what else to do, her hand joined his, kneading the knotted flesh that had cramped so viciously. She could feel the muscles relax when the spasm passed.

"What happened? Did I do something?"

"No." He moved away from her, reaching for the ropes, preparing to raise the sails.

"Talk to me, for heaven's sake," she cried, grabbing his forearm. "Don't close up on me now. I care about you, Jonas, I want to help!"

His hard gaze softened, and he tenderly cupped her cheek. Relieved, Stephanie turned her face into his palm and kissed him there.

"Did I frighten you?" he asked her softly.

"Only because I didn't know what to do to help you." She sighed, feeling weak and emotionally drained. "Does that happen often?" The thought of him enduring such pain was intolerable.

"It happens often enough to make me appreciate my cane."

In spite of the circumstances, Stephanie bowed her head to hide a smile.

"You find that amusing?"

Her head shot up. "No, of course not. It's just that everyone in the office claims they know when your leg is hurting, because you're usually in a foul mood."

"They say that, do they?"

"It's true, isn't it?"

Jonas shrugged. "To be honest, I hadn't given it much thought."

Stephanie reached inside the picnic basket for the two loaves of bread. She set them out along with a plate of cheese, avoiding looking at Jonas as she asked him the question that had been on her mind since Paris. "How'd it happen?"

"My leg?" His gaze sharpened.

"You don't have to tell me if you'd rather not."

He hesitated, and when he finally spoke, Stephanie realized that relating the story to her was an indication that he trusted her. "It happened several years ago in a skiing accident. I was on the slopes with a...friend. There isn't much to say. She got in trouble, and when I went to help her, I fell."

"Down the slope?"

"No, off a cliff."

"Oh, Jonas." She felt sick at the thought of him being hurt. She closed her eyes to the mental image of him lying in some snowbank in agony, waiting for help to arrive.

"The doctors say I'm lucky to have this leg. In the beginning, I wished they had amputated it and been done with it. Now I'm more tolerant of the pain; I've learned to live with it." He grew silent, and Stephanie sensed that there was a great deal more to the story that he hadn't revealed, but she accepted what he had told her and didn't press him further.

"Thank you, Jonas," she said softly.

"For what?"

"For bringing me with you today. For relating what must be a difficult story for you to tell. For trusting me."

"No, Stephanie," he whispered, lifting her mouth to his. "Thank you."

When Jonas pulled up to the large two-story brick home overlooking Lake Superior, Stephanie's breath caught at the sight of his magnificent family home. "Oh, Jonas," she said, awed. "It's beautiful." Imposing as well, she thought, attempting to subdue her nervousness. Her hand went to her hair, and she ran her fingers through the tangled mass.

"You look fine," Jonas told her.

She lowered her arm and rested her clenched hand in her lap. "Just you wait," she threatened. "I'm going to introduce you to my father, and he'll be in mud-spattered coveralls, sitting on top of a tractor. You'll be in a five-hundred-dollar pin-striped suit, and you'll know what it feels like to be out of your element."

To her amazement, Jonas laughed. He parked the car at the front of the house, or perhaps the back—Stephanie couldn't tell which—and turned off the engine. "I'll look forward to meeting your family."

"You will?"

He climbed out of the car and came around to her side, opening her door for her. "One thing, though."

"Yes?"

"Don't introduce me to your mother at Christmas. I have a heck of a time dealing with crying women."

Stephanie got the giggles. They were probably a result of her nervousness, but once she started it was nearly impossible to stop. Jonas laughed with her, and with his arm linked around her waist, he led her through the wide double doors of the house.

The minute they were inside, Stephanie's amusement vanished. The floor of the entryway had probably cost more than her family's farm in Colville. Marble, Stephanie guessed, and probably imported from Italy. Maybe Greece. A large winding stairway angled off to the right; its polished mahogany balustrade gleamed in the sun.

"Jonas, is that you?" An elegantly dressed woman appeared. She was tall and regal-looking, with twinkling blue eyes that were the mirror image of Jonas's. Her hair was completely gray, and she wore it in a neatly coiled French roll. She held her hands out to her son. Jonas claimed them with his own and kissed her on the cheek.

"Mother."

They parted, and Jonas's mother paused to greet Stephanie. If she disapproved of Stephanie's attire, it wasn't revealed in the warmth of her smile. "You must be Stephanie."

For one crazy second, Stephanie had the urge to curtsy. "Hello, Mrs. Lockwood." Even her voice sounded awed and a bit unnatural.

"Please call me Elizabeth."

"Thank you, I will."

"I can see you've had a full day on the lake." Elizabeth glanced at her son.

"It was marvelous," Stephanie confirmed.

"I hope you're hungry. Clara's been cooking all day, anticipating your arrival."

Jonas placed his hand along the back of Stephanie's neck and directed her into the largest room she had ever seen.

"Who's Clara?" she asked under her breath.

"The cook," he whispered. When his mother turned her back, he kissed Stephanie's cheek.

"Jonas," she hissed. "Don't do that!"

"Did you say something, Stephanie?" Elizabeth turned around questioningly.

"Actually...no," she stuttered, glowering hotly at Jonas who coughed to disguise a laugh. "I didn't say anything."

"Would either of you care for a glass of wine before dinner?" Elizabeth asked, taking a seat on an elegant velvet sofa.

Stephanie claimed the matching chair across from her, and Jonas stood behind Stephanie.

"That would be fine, Mother," Jonas said, answering for them both. "Would you like me to serve as bartender?"

"Please." Elizabeth folded her hands on her lap. "Jonas has spoken highly of you, Stephanie."

"He . . . has?" she sputtered.

"Yes, is there something unusual about that?"

Jonas delivered a glass of wine to his mother before bringing Stephanie hers. He sat beside her on the arm of the chair and looped his arm around her shoulder.

"Clara will never forgive you if you don't say hello, Son," Elizabeth informed him. "While you do that, I'll show Stephanie my garden. It's lovely this time of year."

"I'd like that," Stephanie said, standing. She continued to hold her wine, although she had no intention of drinking it. All she needed was to get tipsy in front of Jonas's mother.

"I'll be back in a minute," Jonas whispered as he left the room.

A small, awkward silence followed. Stephanie looked down at her soiled jeans and cringed inwardly. "I feel I should apologize for my attire," Stephanie began, following Jonas's mother out through the French doors that led to a lush green garden. Roses were in bloom, and their sweet fragrance filled the air.

"Nonsense," Elizabeth countered. "You'd been sailing. I didn't expect you to arrive in diamonds and mink."

"But I don't imagine you expected jeans and purple tennis shoes either."

Elizabeth laughed; the sound was light and musical. "I believe I'm going to grow fond of you."

"I hope so." Stephanie studied her wine.

"Forgive me for being so blunt, but are you in love with my son?"

Stephanie raised her eyes to Jonas's mother's and nodded. "Yes."

Elizabeth placed her hand over her heart and sighed expressively. "I am so relieved to hear you say that."

"You are?"

"He loves you, child."

Stephanie opened her mouth to argue, but Elizabeth stopped her.

"I don't know if he's admitted it to himself yet, but he will soon. A few minutes ago, when you came into the house, I heard Jonas laugh. It's been years since I've heard the sound of my son's laughter. Thank you for that."

"Really, I didn't do anything . . . I—"

"Please forgive me for interrupting, but we haven't much time."

Stephanie's heart shot to her throat. "Yes?"

"You must be patient with my son. He's been hurt terribly, and he is greatly in need of a woman's love. He probably hasn't told you about Gretchen; he loved her deeply, far more than the wretched soul deserved. She left him after the accident; she told him she couldn't live with a cripple, even though it was she who had caused it with her carelessness."

Jonas's mother didn't need to say a word more for Stephanie to hate the fickle, faceless woman.

"That was nearly ten years ago, and Jonas hasn't brought another woman to meet me until today. Knowing my son the way I do, I'm sure he'll battle what he feels for you; he's reluctant to trust again. So you must be patient and, my dear," she added, gently touching Stephanie's hand, "be very strong. He deserves your love, and although he may be stubborn now and again, believe me, the woman my son loves will be the happiest woman alive. When Jonas loves again, I promise you it will be with all his heart and his soul."

Stephanie felt fresh tears gather in her eyes. "I don't know if I deserve someone as good as Jonas."

"Perhaps not," Elizabeth Lockwood said, her soft voice cutting any harshness from her words. "But he deserves you." She glanced over her shoulder. "He's coming now, so smile, and please don't say anything about our conversation."

"I won't," Stephanie promised, blinking back tears.

"There you are," Jonas said as he joined his mother and Stephanie. "Did mother let you in on any family secrets?"

"Several, as a matter of fact," Elizabeth said with a small laugh.

"Clara wants me to tell you that dinner is ready any time you are."

"Great," Elizabeth replied with a warm smile.

"She cooked my favorite dessert," Jonas said, sharing a secret smile with Stephanie. "Strawberry shortcake."

Stephanie could feel the heated color seep up her neck, invading her cheeks.

"I don't recall you being particularly fond of strawberries," Elizabeth commented as she led the way into the dining room.

"I am now, Mother," Jonas said, reaching for Stephanie's hand and linking her fingers with his. He raised her knuckles to his mouth and lightly kissed them.

The meal was one Stephanie would long remember, but not because the food could have been served in a four-star restaurant. Jonas was a different person, chatting, joking, teasing. He insisted that Clara join them for coffee so that Stephanie could meet the family cook. Although Stephanie liked the rotund woman instantly, she could feel the older woman's censure. But by the end of the evening, all that had changed and Stephanie knew she could count Clara as a friend.

When it came time to leave, Elizabeth hugged Stephanie and whispered softly in her ear. "Thank you, my dear, for giving me back my son. Remember what I said. Be patient."

"No. Thank *you*," Stephanie whispered back. They joined hands, and Stephanie nodded once. "I'll remember."

It was dark by the time they left Duluth, and Stephanie was physically drained from the long day. She yawned once and tried to disguise it. "I like your family, Jonas."

"They seemed to be quite taken with you."

They talked a bit more, and Stephanie began to drop off, giving way to her fatigue. Jonas woke her when they reached the outskirts of Minneapolis.

"I'm sorry to be such terrible company," she said, yawning.

"You're anything but," Jonas murmured, contradicting her. He eased to a stop in front of her apartment building and parked the car, but kept the engine running.

"Do you want to come in for coffee?" Stephanie invited.

"No, you're exhausted, and I have some work that I need to look over."

"Jonas, don't tell me you're going to work now." She glanced at her wristwatch, shocked to find that it was after eleven.

He chuckled, and leaned over to press his mouth lightly to hers. "No, but it was the best excuse I could come up with to refuse your invitation."

"Good, I was worried there for a minute. You work too hard." She yearned to tell him how much the day had meant to her, how much she'd enjoyed the time on the sailboat and meeting his mother and Clara. But finding the right words was impossible. "Thank you for everything," she said when he helped her out of the car. "I can't remember a day I've enjoyed more."

"Me either," Jonas murmured, his gaze holding hers. "Not in years."

"We've got it!" Jan announced Monday morning, as she, Maureen, Toni and Barbara circled Stephanie's desk like warriors surrounding a wagon train.

"Got what?" Stephanie looked up blankly. She'd only arrived at the office a few minutes before, and hadn't even turned on her typewriter. "What are you talking about?"

"Your move with Mr. Lockwood."

"Oh, that," she returned with a sigh. She hadn't told her friends about the weekend sailing jaunt, but then she'd been keeping quite a few secrets from them lately.

"We've got it all worked out."

"Answer me this first," Stephanie said. "Will I need to wear a cast? Date someone's brother-in-law? Hire a French chef?"

"No."

"It's working out great. We've got a contact in the janitorial department."

"A what?"

"All you have to do," Maureen explained excitedly, "is get in the elevator alone with Mr. Lockwood."

"Yes?" Stephanie could feel the enthusiasm coming from her coworkers in waves. "What will that do?"

"That's where Mike from maintenance comes into the picture," Toni explained patiently.

"He'll flip the switch, and the two of you will be trapped alone together for hours."

"Isn't that a marvelous idea?" Barbara said.

"It works in all the best romances."

"It's a sure thing."

"You're game, aren't you, Steph?"

Chapter Nine

No, I'm not game for your crazy schemes," Stephanie informed her friends primly. It wasn't that she objected to being alone with Jonas for hours on end—that she would relish—but to plot their meeting this way went against everything she hoped for in their relationship.

Jan, Maureen, Toni and Barbara exchanged an incredulous look.

"But it's perfect."

"Jonas and I don't need it," Stephanie said, knowing that the best way to appease her friends was with the truth.

"What do you mean, you don't need it?" Jan asked, her eyes narrowing with suspicion.

"You been holding out on us, girl?" Maureen barked, her hand on her hip.

"I do believe she has," Barbara said before Stephanie had a chance to answer.

"Let's just say this," Stephanie said with a conspiratorial smile. "The romantic relationship between Mr. Lockwood and me is developing nicely."

"How nicely?" Jan wanted to know. "And put it into terms we understand."

"Like on a scale of one to ten," Barbara added.

"What's a ten?" Stephanie glanced up at her friends, uncertain.

"If you need to ask, we're in trouble."

"Right." Hot color blossomed in Stephanie's cheeks.

"If he phoned once or twice and showed up at your apartment—that's a four, a low four."

"But if you shared a couple of romantic evenings on the town, I'd call that a six."

"I'd say meeting his family is an eight," Toni murmured thoughtfully, her index finger pressed against her face. "Maybe a nine."

The four romantics paused expectantly, waiting for Stephanie to gauge her relationship with Jonas on their makeshift scale. "Well?" Jan coaxed.

"An eight then, maybe a nine," she admitted softly, waiting for her friends to break into shouts and cheers. Instead, she was greeted with a shocked, dubious silence.

"You're not teasing, are you!" There was no hint of a question in Barbara's murmured words. "You really aren't joking."

"No. Jonas introduced me to his mother this weekend. She's a wonderful woman."

"It's going to work," Maureen whispered in awe, her face revealing her surprise. "It's really going to work!"

"Speaking of work," Stephanie said pointedly, glancing at her watch. She was relieved not to be subjected to an endless list of questions from her co-workers, but she was so grateful to her romance-loving friends that she wanted them to share some of her happiness.

As though in a daze, Jan, Maureen, Toni and Barbara turned away from her desk. Each walked in short, measured steps, as if in a trance.

"Do you think Mike will give us a refund?" Barbara asked no one in particular as they moved out the door.

"Who cares?" came the reply from the others.

Stephanie's boss, George Potter, arrived at the office a couple of minutes later, having recently returned from Seattle. They exchanged a few pleasantries, and Mr. Potter handed Stephanie some notes from his briefcase. "If you get the chance, could you type these up and give them to Donald Black?"

He said the name of his counterpart stiffly; Stephanie knew from experience that there was little love lost between the two men. Stephanie couldn't imagine her amiable boss disliking anyone, and attributed the low-grade hostility to a personality conflict.

"I can type those right away," she said with a welcoming smile. There was so much to be happy about now and she felt like humming love songs as her fingers flew across the keyboard. She wondered briefly how Jonas's day was going, her thoughts often wandering to the president of Lockwood Industries, who just happened to be in sole possession of her heart.

The morning whizzed past. Stephanie was so close to finishing typing up her boss's notes that she skipped her midmorning coffee break. Five minutes after everyone else had deserted her floor, she pulled the last sheet from her typewriter and sighed. The scribbled notes made for dry reading. She neatly stacked the last page with the others and inserted them into a crisp new file folder.

Mr. Potter was in a meeting, so Stephanie walked down the hallway to give the papers to Donald Black, who was the head of the accounting department.

"Good morning, Mr. Black," she said, knocking politely on his open door. "Mr. Potter asked me to bring these over."

"Put them over there," he said, indicating a table on the other side of the room.

Stephanie placed the file folder where he'd requested and turned to leave, but the middle-aged, potbellied man blocked her way.

"Aren't you and Jonas Lockwood seeing a great deal of each other?"

A plethora of possible answers crowded the end of Stephanie's tongue. Jonas had mentioned that he'd prefer to keep their personal relationship out of the office, but Stephanie wasn't in the habit of lying. Nor was it her custom to discuss her personal relationships with a stranger.

"We're . . . friends," she said, believing that Jonas himself must have mentioned her to the other man.

"I see." With slow, deliberate movements, Donald placed his pencil on the edge of the file he was reading. "How willing are you to be... friends with other Lockwood employees?"

Stephanie stiffened at the insulting way he uttered the word *friends*. "I'm not sure I understand the question."

"I'm quite certain you do."

Stephanie didn't know what type of games this middle-aged Don Juan was playing, but she had no intention of remaining in his office. "If you'll excuse me."

"As a matter of fact, I won't. We're having an important discussion here, and I'd consider it a desertion of your duties to this company and to me personally if you left."

Stephanie wasn't much into the office gossip, but she was aware that George Potter had no respect for Donald Black. As the head of the accounting department, he'd been through three secretaries in the two years Stephanie had been employed by Lockwood Industries. From her own dismal experience with her former employers, she could guess the reason Donald Black had trouble keeping a decent secretary.

"I'll desert my duties then," she replied flippantly. She turned to go, but didn't make it to the door. His hand reached out and gripped her shoulder, spinning her around. Stephanie was so shocked that he would dare to touch her that she was momentarily speechless.

"Everyone in the company knows you're being generous with Lockwood. All I want is a share in the goods."

Still breathless with shock, Stephanie slapped his hand aside. "You sicken me."

"Give me time, honey, I promise to improve."

"I sincerely doubt that." He grasped her by the shoulders then, intent on kissing her, but Stephanie managed to evade him. With everything that was in her, she pushed against his chest with both hands and was astonished at the strength of the man.

Her eye happened to catch the clock, and Stephanie realized it would be another five minutes before anyone returned to the department. Crying out would do no good, since there wasn't anyone there to answer her plea for help.

"All I want is a little kiss," Donald said coaxingly. "Just give me that and I'll let you go."

"I'd rather vomit," she cried, kicking at him and missing.

"You stupid—"

"Let her go."

The quietly spoken words evidenced such controlled anger that both Stephanie and her attacker froze. Donald dropped his arms and released her.

With a strangled sob, Stephanie turned aside and braced her hands against the edge of the desk, weak with relief. Her neatly coiled hair had fallen free of its restraining pins, and hung in loose tendrils around her flushed face. It took her several deep breaths to regain her strength. She didn't know how or why Jonas was here, but she had never been so glad to see anyone.

"Clear out your desk, Black." The emotionless, frigid control in Jonas's voice brought a chill to Stephanie's spine. She'd never heard a man more angry and more dangerous. Acid dripped from each syllable. An unspoken challenge hung over the room almost as if Jonas welcomed a physical confrontation.

"Hey, Jonas, you got the wrong idea here. Your lady friend came on to me." Black raised both hands in an emotional plea of innocence.

Stephanie spun around, her eyes spitting fire.

"Is that true?" Jonas asked evenly.

"No," she shouted, indignant and furious. "He grabbed me—"

"You didn't hear her crying out, did you?" Black shot back, interrupting Stephanie. "I swear, man, I'm not the kind of guy who has to force women. They come to me."

"I said clear out your desk." Jonas pointed the tip of his cane at the far door. "A check will be mailed to you tomorrow."

Donald Black gave Stephanie a murderous glare as he marched out of the office. "You'll regret this, Lockwood," he muttered on his way past Jonas.

Stephanie could see the coiled alertness drain from Jonas the minute Black was out of the room. "Did he hurt you?"

"No...I'm fine." Stephanie closed her eyes. She was too proud to allow a man like Donald Black to reduce her to tears.

Jonas's arm came around her, comforting and warm, chasing away the icy, numbing chill that had settled over her. "I'm fine," she whispered fiercely, burying her face in his shoulder. "Really."

"Let's get out of here." Jonas led her into the hallway and toward the elevator. Stephanie didn't recall any of the ride to the top floor, but when the thick door glided open, Jonas called to Bertha Westheimer.

"Bring me a strong cup of coffee, and add plenty of sugar."

"Jonas, really," Stephanie insisted, her voice wavering slightly. "I'm fine, and I'm certainly not anywhere near being in shock."

He ignored her, leading her into his office and sitting her down in a thick leather chair. He paced the area directly in front of her until his ever-efficient secretary appeared with the coffee, carefully handing it to Stephanie. The older woman gave Stephanie a sympathetic look that puzzled Stephanie. She couldn't understand why the other woman would regard her with such compassion, but then she remembered her hair. She smiled back as Bertha quietly left the room, softly closing the door behind her.

"I won't ever have you subjected to that kind of treatment again," Jonas roared, still battling his anger.

Stephanie stared up at him blankly as he paced. He marched like a soldier doing sentry duty, going three or four feet, then swiftly making a sharp about-face. She realized his irritation wasn't directed at her.

"We're getting married," he announced forcefully.

Stephanie's immediate response was to take a sip of the syrupy coffee, convinced she'd misunderstood him.

"Well?" he barked.

"Would you mind repeating the question...I'm certain I heard you wrong."

"I said we're getting married." He said it louder this time.

Stephanie blinked twice. "If I wasn't in shock before, I am now. You can't possibly mean that, Jonas."

"My name will protect you."

"But, Jonas—"

"Will or won't you be my wife?" he yelled.

"Stop shouting at me," she cried, jumping to her feet. The coffee nearly sloshed over the edges of the Styrofoam cup, and Stephanie set it down before she ended up spilling it down the front of her dress.

"Anything could have happened down there," Jonas continued. "If I hadn't arrived when I did..." He left the rest to her imagination.

Stephanie went still, her gaze studying this man she loved. "Isn't marriage a little drastic?"

"Not in these circumstances." He looked at her as though she were the one being unreasonable.

"Jonas, do you love me?" she asked the question softly, almost fearing his response.

"I'd hardly be willing to make you my wife if I didn't."

"I see."

He hesitated, looking uneasy. "How do you feel about me?"

"Oh, Jonas, do you really need to ask?" Her gaze softened, and her heart melted at the pride and doubt she read in his hard expression. He was more vulnerable now than at any time since she'd begun working for him. "I've been in love with you from the moment we stood in front of the fountain in Paris—only it took a while to realize it."

His eyes looked deeply into hers, and when he spoke, the burning anger had been replaced by tenderness. "Stephanie, I love you. I didn't ever expect to fall so hard, and certainly not for a tiny slip of a woman who is so proud and forthright. But it's happened, and I'll thank God every day of my life if you'll agree to marry me and have my children.''

"Oh, Jonas.'' She cupped her hand over her mouth and battled back the tidal wave of emotion that threatened to engulf her. Then she sniffled and turned around, desperately seeking a tissue.

Jonas handed her one and paused to cup her face in his hands. He smiled at her gently, lovingly. "We're going to have a wonderful life together,'' he said as he lowered his mouth to hers. His kiss was tender and sweet, and his tongue probed her mouth with slow, easy thrusts that made Stephanie's knees grow weak.

Her arms curled and locked around his neck as his mouth meandered over her lips to her ear. "You're a crazy woman.''

"Crazy about you,'' she admitted, loving the feel of him rubbing against her, knowing that their lovemaking would be exquisite.

"A man attacks you and you're a fireball. I ask you to marry me, and you burst into tears.''

"I'm happy.''

"You will, won't you?''

"Marry you? Oh, Jonas, I'd consider it the greatest honor of my life to be your wife.''

"You won't mind children?''

"A dozen at least,'' she said with a happy laugh. Fresh tears misted her eyes at the thought of bearing Jonas's child.

"A dozen?'' He cocked his brows and grinned sheepishly. "I'm willing, but you may want to change your mind after three or four.'' Still holding her, Jonas flipped the switch to the intercom. "Miss West-heimer?''

"Yes," came the tinny-sounding reply.

"Contact Mr. Potter and tell him that Miss Coulter won't be in for the remainder of the day."

"Jonas," Stephanie whispered. "I told you Black didn't hurt me. I'm fine, really."

He ignored her, but his grip on her shoulder tightened. "And cancel my appointments for today as well."

"Yes, of course," the secretary said, but the reluctance in her voice was evident even to Stephanie.

"Is that a problem, Miss Westheimer?"

"Adam Holmes is scheduled for four-thirty, and he'll be leaving town this evening," Bertha informed her employer in the same dry tone.

Jonas closed his eyes and sighed with frustration. "All right, I'll make a point of being back before four-thirty, then."

When he'd finished speaking, he released the switch and turned Stephanie into his arms. "We have some shopping to do."

"Shopping?" For some reason her mind flashed to the grocery store. She hadn't eaten breakfast, and had hoped to pick up something easy on her coffee break, but she'd been so involved typing the report that she'd forgotten.

"Shopping for a ring. A diamond, preferably, and so large anyone looking at it will know how special you are and how much I love you."

"Jonas," she said slowly, measuring her words carefully, "a plain gold band would do as long as I'm marrying you."

"I can afford a whole lot more, and I have every intention of indulging you from this minute to the end of our lives."

Stephanie swallowed her objections; she loved Jonas, and not for the material wealth he could give her. She remembered Elizabeth Lockwood's words. Jonas's mother had told her that when Jonas admitted that he loved her, he would make her the happiest woman alive. For now he equated bringing her joy with adorning her with riches. Diamonds were wonderful, but Stephanie's happiness came from being loved by Jonas and nothing more. It wouldn't matter to her if he sold matchsticks on street corners; she loved the man. In time, he'd learn that her happiness was linked to his. He was all she'd ever need to be content and whole.

His look grew sober and thoughtful. "What do you think about making Potter a first vice president?"

Stephanie was both stunned and thrilled. She was surprised that Jonas was considering such a move, and complimented that he would ask her opinion. "George Potter is a wonderful choice."

"Then consider it done," Jonas said with a curt nod. "Now that I'm going to be a married man, I don't want to spend so much time at the office. Not when I have more important matters to concern myself with."

"Right," she said with a wide grin, thinking of all the years they'd have to build a life together. She could see them thirty-five years from now, teaching their grandchildren to sail. "Jonas," she said suddenly, remembering her own happy childhood. "I want you to meet my parents and my sisters."

"We can fly out next week," he answered matter-of-factly.

"When do you want to have the wedding?" she asked. Jonas was moving so fast he was making her head spin.

"Is next month too soon?"

"Oh, Jonas," she cried, wrapping her arms around his neck and hugging him fiercely. "I wonder if it will be near soon enough."

From that point, the afternoon took on the feel of a circus ride. Their first stop was the jeweler's, where Jonas bought a lovely diamond solitaire. When he slipped it on her finger, Stephanie felt the tears gather in her eyes. She bit into her lower lip to keep them at bay, not wanting to embarrass either of them with her emotional display. From the jeweler's, Jonas drove to an exclusive French restaurant in memory of their trip to Paris. They dined on veal, sipped champagne, and shared secret glances with eyes full of love.

At four, Jonas glanced irritably at his watch. "I may be tied up with Holmes for several hours, and then I've got a dinner engagement."

"Not with another woman, I hope," Stephanie teased.

He looked startled for a moment. "There'll never be another woman for me, Stephanie. Never."

"Jonas, I was only joking."

"You need never doubt me on this, Stephanie. All my life I've been intensely loyal. I'm sure my mother can give you several examples from my boyhood if you want to hear them."

"Jonas, please, I didn't mean to imply..."

"I know, love." He paused to caress the side of her face tenderly. "I knew I was falling in love with you, perhaps even as early as Paris, but I fought it. I thought I was in love once before, and I was thoroughly disgusted with the emotion. But this morning, when I saw Black pawing at you—I've never experienced such overwhelming rage. I knew in that moment that the feelings I hold for you could be nothing less than love."

Her hand found his and squeezed it gently. "Having you love me is the greatest honor I've ever known."

Jonas's blue eyes darkened by several shades, and Stephanie realized that had they been anywhere other than a restaurant, he would have taken her in his arms and kissed her until she begged him to stop.

From the restaurant, Jonas drove her back to the office building with him. Stephanie was about to burst with happiness, and if she didn't share it with Jan and the others soon, she was convinced she'd start screaming that Jonas Lockwood loved her from the top floor for all Minneapolis to hear.

Her first stop after she and Jonas parted at the elevator was the personnel office. Jan looked up from her desk and blinked.

"Hey, where were you at lunchtime? I have a feeling you were trying to avoid questions. You can't do this to us, Steph, we're all dying to find out what's happening."

"I wasn't avoiding anyone."

Jan looked at her more intently. "You've got that saucy grin again. Would you care to tell me the reason you look like a contented cat with feathers in his mouth?''

In response, Stephanie held out her left hand. The large diamond solitaire sparkled merrily in the artificial light.

Jan gasped, and her eyes shot to Stephanie's. "Mr. Lockwood?"

"Who else would it be?"

Jan's palm flew to her breast. "I think I'm going into cardiac arrest. You did it! You actually did it!" Even as she spoke, she was reaching for the phone.

"Tell the others to meet us at that cocktail lounge you took me to that night. The drinks are on me this time," Stephanie said happily. "I owe all of you at least that."

An hour later, the five were gathered around a table, sipping wine coolers and munching on an assortment of chips, deep-fried zucchini sticks, and mushrooms stuffed with cheese and onions.

"How did you get him to propose?" Barbara wanted to know first.

"I didn't do anything. I was more surprised than any of you."

Jan refilled Stephanie's glass, and they all raised their drinks in a silent salute to their illustrious boss.

"To years and years of happiness," Maureen said, offering the toast.

"And romance," Stephanie added, a believer now. She recalled the first time she'd met with her co-workers and how they'd claimed then to have recognized her as the perfect match for Jonas Lockwood. At the time, Stephanie had been shocked, even appalled. She wouldn't have given the man a free bus ticket. Now, at the very mention of his name, her knees turned to butter, she was so much in love with him. Truly head over heels in love, for the first time in her life.

"Who guessed today?" Toni questioned.

"No one," Jan answered. "Remember, it was as much a surprise to Steph as it is to us."

"Today? What today?" Stephanie glanced around the table at her friends. True, they'd all had their share of wine, Stephanie a bit more than her share since she'd also had champagne at lunch with Jonas. But until this moment, everything her friends had said made perfect sense.

"I guess we'll have to award the three hundred dollars to the one who guesses the correct wedding day."

"Would you stop talking in riddles," Stephanie demanded.

"Have you decided on a date for the wedding yet?"

Stephanie noticed how intense the four faces became as they awaited her reply. "I'm not answering your question until you answer mine," she said, crossing her arms stubbornly. "What's all this about guessing the day?"

"The marriage pool."

"The what?" Stephanie cried.

"You know, like a football pool, only we had bets going on when Lockwood was going to pop the question."

Stephanie took another swallow of her wine cooler. "I can't believe I'm hearing this."

"A lot of people bet that you wouldn't be able to carry this off. They lost this big." Jan and Maureen slapped hands high above the table.

"Money?"

"Three hundred dollars is riding on your wedding date."

Stephanie placed her elbows on the table and cradled her head in her hands. "So that's where Black heard about me and Jonas," she mumbled under her breath.

"Say, do you know what happened to him today?"

"How would I know?" Stephanie didn't look her friend in the eye, her gaze fixed on the ice floating in her drink. She hoped that by asking, she could avoid lying.

"I got a call from Old Stone Face shortly after I returned from coffee break this morning. She told me that Donald Black had been terminated, and to arrange for his check to be mailed to him at his home."

"How unusual," Stephanie commented, struggling not to reveal any of her involvement with the decision.

"I don't know anyone who's sorry to see him go," Maureen added. "He was a real—"

"We know what he was," Toni inserted quickly.

"Did anything else of importance occur today?" Stephanie hoped to steer the conversation away from any more unpleasant subjects.

"You mean other than you and Mr. Lockwood getting engaged, and Donald Black biting the dust? I'd say that was enough to make it one hell of a Monday."

"Can you imagine what Tuesday's going to be like?" Maureen asked. They all giggled, knowing nothing could outdo the events of this day.

From the cocktail lounge, the five went to dinner at a Mexican restaurant, and by the time Stephanie got home it was close to ten. She hoped Jonas hadn't tried to get in touch with her, and felt a little guilty for staying out so late. As it was, her head was swimming, and she took a quick shower and hurried to bed.

The following morning she was at her desk bright and early, hoping Jonas would stop in on his way up to his floor. She didn't know how she was going to be able to work when all she could think about was how much she loved Jonas and how eager she was to share his life.

Before George Potter arrived, Stephanie received a call from Jan. "Can you come to personnel?"

"Sure, what's up? You don't sound right."

"Just get here."

Stephanie couldn't understand why her friend should sound so upset, and she hurried to the personnel office. She took one look at Jan's red eyes and grew worried. Her friend reached for a tissue and loudly blew her nose.

"What's wrong?" Stephanie asked, taking a chair. She'd never seen Jan cry. Her friend must be terribly upset.

"Mr. Lockwood contacted me first thing this morning."

"Jonas?"

"You've been terminated."

Alarm filled Stephanie for an instant, but then she sighed and offered Jan a reassuring grin. "Of course, I have. Jonas and I are getting married. I can't very well continue to work here." They hadn't talked about it specifically, but Stephanie was sure that was it.

"I don't think so," Jan said. She reached for another tissue, blinking back fresh tears.

"You're not making any sense. What else did Jonas say?"

He said..." She paused to wipe her eyes. "He said to mail you your check just the way I was instructed to do with Mr. Black, and ... and he asked that you give me the engagement ring. He doesn't want you on Lockwood property again. He was clear as glass on that subject."

Stephanie felt as though someone had kicked her in the stomach. For a moment she couldn't breathe. Her heart constricted with an intolerable pain.

"Steph, did you hear me?"

She nodded numbly. "Why?" The word came from deep within her throat, low and guttural.

"He...he didn't say, but he was serious, Steph. Very serious. I've never heard him more angry. You'd better give me the ring."

Chapter Ten

Stephanie's right hand covered the large diamond engagement ring protectively. "I don't understand it. Jonas isn't making sense."

"He was very precise when he contacted me."

Pacing the carpet in front of Jan's desk, Stephanie folded her arms around her waist and pondered her friend's words. "Contact Barbara, Toni and Maureen, and ask them to come to personnel right away."

"What?"

"Just do it," Stephanie snapped, impatient now. "And tell them to hurry."

Momentarily dumbfounded, Jan hesitated, then reached for the phone. The contacts were made in a matter of minutes, and one by one her three co-workers rushed into the personnel office.

"What is it?" Maureen asked breathlessly, the first to arrive.

Toni followed on her heels. "Hey, what's so important?"

Barbara sauntered in last, paused, glanced around and said, "All right, I'm here, what's the big deal?"

Jan gestured toward Stephanie. "You called them here; you explain."

"Apparently," Stephanie began, swallowing the thickening in her throat, "Jonas wants to call off the engagement."

"What?" Three discordant voices cried out in disbelief.

Barbara recovered first. "What happened?"

"I...don't know," Stephanie admitted honestly, her stomach churning as she considered the incredible situation. "I arrived at the office this morning, and Jan contacted me. She told me I had been terminated by Lockwood Industries, and I was to return the engagement ring to her."

Simultaneously Barbara, Toni and Maureen turned accusing eyes on Jan.

"Hey," Jan said, slapping her chest. "It wasn't my fault. I'm as shocked as the rest of you."

Stephanie twisted the diamond around and around on her finger, believing that she'd almost prefer to lose the appendage than surrender the ring that had been a token of Jonas's love. "You four are the self-proclaimed experts on love. You're the ones who convinced me that Jonas and I were meant for each other. I need your advice now more than ever." Stephanie spoke quietly, doing her best to keep the emotion from her voice. "What can I do now?"

"Did he give any reason?"

"None," Jan answered. "But he was so angry...worse than I can ever remember hearing him."

"Can you think of anything?" Maureen turned to Stephanie, her brow creased in a frown that revealed the depth of her bafflement.

"Nothing. Absolutely nothing." She turned her palms to them in a gesture indicating her own confusion. Unless Donald Black had somehow convinced Jonas that she hadn't been speaking the truth...but that wasn't possible, Stephanie decided. Jonas knew her better than that. At least she prayed he did.

"Are you going to give him back the ring?" Toni asked quietly, her voice dejected and unhappy.

"I...don't know yet."

"It's obvious he doesn't want to face you," Jan said, her expression thoughtful.

"Probably because he's afraid of what would happen."

"But I would never hurt him," Stephanie returned, appalled at the suggestion that she would do anything to cause Jonas pain.

"Not physically, silly," Barbara explained with a long sigh. "It's obvious that he loves you—that isn't going to change overnight—so breaking off the engagement is bound to be emotionally painful."

"Maybe even impossible, if he's forced to face you."

"Then that's exactly what's going to happen." For the first time, Stephanie thought she could see a glimmer of hope. She wouldn't make things easy for Jonas. "I'm not going to hand over this ring without an explanation."

"You shouldn't," Maureen stated emphatically.

"He isn't going to let it happen."

"He isn't?" Stephanie wasn't nearly as convinced as her friends.

"Oh, he might let you get as far as the door—"

"Maybe even the elevator," Jan interrupted.

"But he'll come for you once he realizes you really mean to leave."

"He'll stop me?" Stephanie was doubtful.

"Oh yes, the hero always rejects the heroine, and then at the very last second he realizes that he couldn't possibly live without her."

"He may even quietly plead with you and say 'Don't go' in a tormented voice. You'd be crazy to walk away from him then."

"It's like that in all the best romances," Maureen said, nodding her head sharply.

"But Jonas hasn't read any of those." Stephanie wanted desperately to believe that what her friends said was true, but she was afraid to count on it. Jonas was too proud. Too stubborn. Too Jonas.

"He's enough of a hero to know when he's turning away from the best thing that's ever happened to him. He loves you."

Barbara's words were the cool voice of reason cutting through the fog of doubt that clouded Stephanie's troubled mind. Even Elizabeth Lockwood had told Stephanie how much Jonas needed her love. She couldn't doubt his own mother.

"He must love you, or he wouldn't have asked you to marry him." Toni was equally convincing.

"So the next move is mine, right?" Stephanie glanced around at her friends' intent expressions.

"Most definitely."

The four followed Stephanie out of personnel, moving in single file like troops marching into battle. Down the hallway they paraded, finally coming to a halt in front of the elevator. Jan pushed the button for Stephanie while the others offered words of encouragement.

"Fight for him," Barbara advised her thoughtfully. "If he's going to do this to you, then don't make it easy on him."

"Right," Toni concurred. "Let him know what he's missing."

"Good luck," Jan cried as Stephanie walked into the elevator. Just before the thick steel doors glided shut her friends gave her the thumbs-up sign.

All the confidence Stephanie had felt when she stepped into the elevator deserted her the minute she faced Bertha Westheimer. The woman barely looked in Stephanie's direction. It was apparent the dragon was prepared for this confrontation.

For a full, intolerable minute Stephanie stood in front of the dragon's desk. Bertha ignored her.

"Excuse me, please," Stephanie said in a strong, controlled tone. "I'm here to see Mr. Lockwood."

"He's in a meeting."

"I don't believe that."

"My dear young lady, it is hardly my concern what you believe. Mr. Lockwood has no desire to see you."

"Now, that, I believe."

For the first time since Stephanie had known Jonas's secretary, Bertha Westheimer smiled. Well, almost smiled, Stephanie corrected herself. She wasn't completely convinced that the woman was capable of revealing her amusement.

"I'd like to help you, but . . ."

"I'll simply tell him you weren't able to stop me."

"Mr. Lockwood would know better," Bertha said quietly. "If I can persevere against pesky attorneys and keep persistent salesmen at bay, one female employee is a piece of cake."

But Stephanie could see that Bertha was weakening, which was in itself a sight to behold.

"He's in a rare mood," Bertha whispered under her breath. "I don't remember ever seeing him quite like this."

"Is it his leg?"

"I beg your pardon?" The horn-rimmed glasses that balanced so precariously at the tip of the secretary's nose threatened to slide off. Bertha rescued them in the nick of time. "I don't understand your question."

"Jonas is often irritable and cranky when his leg is hurting him."

"No, it's not his leg, Ms. Coulter. It's you. First thing this morning, I asked about you. When Mr. Lockwood brought you into the office yesterday, it was apparent there'd been some trouble. You were shaking like a frightened rabbit and . . . well, the minute I said your name, Mr. Lockwood nearly bit my head off. He said if I cared about my job I was to forget I'd ever met you. I've been with Mr. Lockwood for a good number of years, and I have never seen him like he was this morning. From the looks of it, I'd say he didn't go home last night."

A sense of urgency filled Stephanie. "It's imperative that I talk to him."

"I have my instructions, but quite honestly, Ms. Coulter, I don't believe I can go through—"

"Ms. Westheimer." Jonas's voice boomed over the intercom, startling both women. "Just how much longer am I to be kept waiting for the Westinghouse file?"

Stephanie's heart pounded frantically at the cold, hard sound of Jonas's voice. She'd thought she'd seen him in every mood imaginable. He could be unreasonable and flippant, but she had never known him to be deliberately cruel. Judging from the edge in his voice, she didn't doubt he was capable of anything this day.

"Right away, sir," Bertha answered quickly. She raised her head and whispered to Stephanie. "It would be better if you came back another day... perhaps tomorrow, when he's had a chance to mull things over."

"No," Stephanie countered, and shook her head for emphasis. "It's now or never." Squaring her shoulders, she picked up the file he'd requested. It was on the corner of Bertha's desk. "I'll take this to him."

Bertha half rose from her chair, indecision etched in her pointed features. "I... can't let you do that."

"You can, and you will," Stephanie told her just as firmly.

Slumping back into her chair, Bertha shook her head slowly and shut her eyes. "I hope I'm doing the right thing."

With her hand on the knob of the door that led to Jonas's office, Stephanie hesitated for a second, then pushed open the door. With quick firm steps, she marched across the plush carpeting and placed the file folder on Jonas's desk. Jonas was busy writing and didn't glance in her direction.

"I believe you asked for this," she said softly.

His head flew up so fast that for a moment she wondered if he'd given himself whiplash.

"Get out!"

The harsh words cut through Stephanie, but she refused to give in to the pain. "Not until you tell me what's going on. Jan Michaels gave me the most ridiculous message this morning. If you want to end our engagement, I have the right to know why."

His finger pointed viciously at the door. "I've had a change of heart. Leave the ring with Ms. Westheimer and get out of my sight."

She winced at the cold, merciless way he looked at her. "It's not that simple, Jonas," she said quietly, fighting back her anger and indignation. "I have a right to know what happened. This doesn't make any sense. One afternoon you love me enough to ask me to share your life, and then you despise me the following morning."

Jonas lowered his gaze, and it looked for a minute as though he was going to snap the pen he was holding in half. His hands clenched and unclenched.

"Does it have anything to do with Donald Black?"

His eyes shot to hers and narrowed. "No, but perhaps I was hasty in firing the man."

Stephanie decided to let that comment slide. "Then what possible explanation could there be?"

He rose slowly from his chair and braced his hands on the side of the desk, leaning forward. His eyes were as blue as a glacier and just as cold. "An interesting thing happened on my way out of the office yesterday afternoon. I heard howls of laughter coming from a group of male employees. By pure chance, I happened to overhear how Stephanie Coulter had managed to pull off the feat of the century. A mere secretary had won the heart of the company president. Apparently some money was riding on just how quickly you could make a fool of me."

Stephanie blanched, wanting to crawl into a hole, shrivel up and die. "Jonas, I . . ."

"I didn't believe it at first," Jonas interjected, his voice as sharp as a new razor blade. "At least not until I saw the betting sheet posted on the bulletin board. You did amazingly well; the odds weren't in your favor. Several of the women seemed to have underestimated you. But I noticed the men were quick to trust your many charms. But only three hundred dollars? Really, Stephanie, you sold yourself cheap."

His eyes narrowed as he mentioned the money, and Stephanie wanted to cry out with rage. "I didn't have anything to do with the marriage pool."

"Not according to what I overheard. You've been in on this little setup from the beginning. You and half the office were plotting my downfall like I was some puppet on a string. Tricking me into falling in love with you was all part of the plan, wasn't it?"

"I—"

"Don't bother to deny it. At least have the decency to own up to the truth."

"I never had any intention of falling in love with you," she admitted, battling back tears.

"I suppose not. All you wanted—all anyone wanted—was to see me make a fool of myself."

Moisture wetted her lashes, but Stephanie refused to give in to the wall of tears that threatened to erupt at any second. "You want the truth, then fine, I'll tell you everything."

Jonas reclaimed his chair and reached for his pen. "I have no desire to hear it."

He started writing, ignoring her, but Stephanie refused to walk away from him now. He had to understand that it had never been a game with her. She'd fallen into the girls' plans as an unwilling victim.

"Several weeks ago, a few of the ladies from the office approached me . . . it was right after I'd worked for you when Ms. Westheimer was ill." She waited for some response, but when Jonas didn't give her any, Stephanie continued undaunted. "They believed . . . the girls from the office . . . that you worked so hard and demanded so much of everyone else because you needed a wife and family to fill your time. They thought you and I were perfect together."

Jonas snickered.

Stephanie did her best to ignore it. "Anyway, I laughed at them and told them it was a crazy idea. I didn't want any part of it."

"Obviously something changed your mind."

"Yes, something did," she cried. "Paris. I met the real Jonas Lockwood at a fountain in a French park, and I knew then that I'd never be the same. For just a fleeting instant, I glimpsed the man inside that thick facade and discovered how much I could come to love him."

"More's the pity."

"I had no intention of falling in love with you. It just . . . happened. Even now, I don't regret it, I can't. I love you, Jonas Lockwood. I apologize that the girls' game got carried to that extent, but please believe me,

I didn't have anything to do with the marriage pool. I didn't even know anything about it until yesterday.'' She paused, her chest heaving with the tension that coiled her insides like a finely tuned violin. ''I'd never do anything to hurt you. Never.''

Jonas dropped his gaze again. ''Okay, you've had your say, and I've listened. It's what you wanted. Now kindly do as I request and leave the diamond with Ms. Westheimer. Whatever was between us, and I sincerely doubt it was love, is over.''

Stephanie felt as though he'd physically struck her. Tears burned in her eyes, brimmed, and fell over the thick lashes onto her cheek. ''You put this ring on my finger,'' she said softly, slowly. ''If you want it off, you'll have to remove it yourself.'' She held her hand out to him, and waited.

Although he refused to look at her, Stephanie could sense his indecision. ''If it isn't love that's between us, I don't know what it is,'' she added softly.

''I saw you last night,'' he said, in a voice so low that the words were barely audible. ''You came out of some cocktail lounge, laughing and joking with a group of women, and I knew it was a victory celebration. You'd achieved the impossible. You'd brought me to my knees.''

''Not that...never that.'' Stephanie didn't know how to explain that she'd simply been happy and had wanted to share her joy with her friends. But words would only condemn her now.

''Keep the diamond,'' he said finally. ''You've earned it.''

''Jonas, please—''

"Either you leave peacefully, or I'll call security and have you thrown out." His tone left little doubt that the threat was real.

Stunned almost to the point of numbness, Stephanie turned away from him. Tears blinded her as she headed for the door. Her hand was on the knob when she paused, not daring to look at him. "Did you say something?" she asked hopefully.

"No."

She nodded and, leaving the door open, moved into the foyer and to the elevator. Something came over her then. A sensation so strong and so powerful that she could barely contain it. With a burst of magnetic energy she whirled around and stormed back into his office, stopping at his desk. "Well," she cried, her hands on her hips. "Aren't you going to stop me?"

Jonas glanced up and snarled. "What the hell are you talking about?"

"They said you'd stop me."

"Who?"

"The girls. They said if you really loved me . . . if anything between us was real, that you wouldn't be such an idiot as to let me leave." She'd improvised a bit, but that had been the gist of their message.

"I can assure you that after yesterday I have no feelings for you. None. At this point, my only intention regarding you is to sever our relationship and be done with you once and for all."

"You fool," she cried, swallowing a hysterical sob. "If your pride is worth so much to you, then fine—so be it. If you want your ring back, then here it is." She paused long enough to slip it off her finger and place it on his desk. "It's over now, and all the trust and

promise that went with it: the love, the joy, the laughter, the home, the family.'' She sucked in her breath at
the unexpected pain that gripped her heart. ''Our
children would have been so special.''

Jonas's mouth went taut, but he said nothing.

''It may surprise you to know that you're not the
only one with an abundance of pride.'' Although she
said each word as clearly as possible, the tears rained
down her face. She turned and pointed to the elevator. ''It's going to tear my heart out to walk out that
door, but I'm going to do it. From here on, you'll live
your life and I'll live mine and we'll probably never
meet again. But I love you, Jonas, I'll always love you.
Not now, and probably not soon, but someday, you'll
regret this. My love will haunt you, Jonas, all the way
to your grave.''

''I suggest if you're going to leave you do it
quickly,'' he said tonelessly, ''before security ar-
rives.''

''Stop trying to hurt me more,'' she shouted, her
voice cracking. ''Isn't this humiliation enough?''

Again he refused to answer her.

''Goodbye, Jonas,'' she said softly, her voice trem-
bling violently. She turned and walked away from him,
telling herself over and over again not to look back. It
wasn't until she was in the elevator that she realized
she was speaking out loud.

As the elevator carried her to the bottom floor,
Stephanie felt as though she were descending into the
depths of hell. She paused in the washroom to wipe the
tears from her face and repair the damage to her
makeup. Unable to face anyone at the moment, she

took the bus directly home and contacted Jan from there.

"What happened?" Jan cried. "Everyone's dying to know."

"The engagement is off," Stephanie announced, doing her utmost to keep her voice from cracking. "I've contacted my parents. I'm letting go of the apartment and flying home at the end of the week. The sooner I leave Minneapolis the better."

"Steph, don't do anything foolish. It'll work out."

"It's not going to resolve itself," she cried, pressing her fist against her forehead. "Jonas made that very clear, and I refuse to remain in this city any longer." Not when there was a chance she'd run into Jonas again. She could bear anything but that.

"I feel terrible," Jan mumbled, "Really terrible—I was the one who got you into this."

"I got myself into it, and no one else. I love him, Jan, and a part of me always will."

"Are you crying?"

"No." Stephanie tried to smile, but the effort was a miserable failure. "The tears are gone now. I'm not saying I didn't cry; believe me, this morning it was Waterworks International around here. But my crying jag is over. I'll recover in time—that's the best thing about being a Coulter—we bounce back." Her mother had reminded her of that, and they'd wept together, paying long-distance rates to do so.

Jan sighed with a hint of envy. "I can't believe you—you're so strong. If this were to happen between me and Jim, I'd come unglued."

Family was the sticking agent that would hold Stephanie together. Her parents would help her get through this ordeal. Now, more than at any time since she'd left home, Stephanie felt the need for the comforting love of her parents and all that was familiar. The wheat farm, the old two-story farmhouse with the wide front porch. The half-mile-long driveway with rolling fields of grain on either side. Home. Family. Love.

"Is there anything I can do for you?" Jan wanted to know next.

"Nothing. If...if I don't see you before Saturday, say goodbye to everyone for me. I'll miss you all."

"Oh, Steph, I hate to see it come to this."

"I do too, but it's for the best."

For four days, Stephanie tried to pick up the pieces of her shattered life. She packed her bags, sold what furniture she could and gave the rest to charity. None of it was worth much, since she'd bought most of it secondhand. The bookcase was the most difficult to part with, and in the end she disassembled it and packed the long boards with the rest of the things she was having trucked to Colville. The expense of doing so was worth more than three similar sets of bookshelves, but this was all that she'd have to remember Jonas by, and even though she was doing everything humanly possible to purge him from her life, she wanted to hang on to the bookcase and the memory of that night together.

Late Friday afternoon, her suitcases resting in the barren apartment, Stephanie waited for Jan to pick her up and drive her to a hotel close to the airport. She half expected Maureen, Toni and Barbara to arrive with Jan, and she mentally braced herself for the drain on her emotions. Goodbyes were always difficult.

When the doorbell chimed, she took a deep breath and attempted to smile brightly.

"Hello, Stephanie." A vital, handsome Jonas stood in the doorway.

"Jonas." Her fingers clutched the doorhandle so tightly that Stephanie thought the knob would break free. All week she'd been praying for a miracle, but had given up hope; Jonas was too proud, and Stephanie knew it.

"May I come in?"

She blinked twice and stepped aside. "As you can see, I can't offer you a seat," she said, leaning against the closed door.

Jonas stepped into the middle of the bare room and whirled around sharply. "You're leaving?"

"I'm expecting my ride in a few minutes—I thought you were Jan."

"I see."

"You wanted something?" She tried to keep the eagerness from her voice. In her dreams, he had had her in his arms by now.

"I've come to offer you your job back."

Her hopeful expectations died a cruel death. "No, thank you."

"Why not?"

"Surely you know the reason, Jonas."

He hesitated, ambled to the other side of the room, and glanced out the window to the street below. "You're a damn good secretary."

Stephanie held her ground. "Then I shouldn't have much problem finding work in Washington."

"I'll double your salary," he said, not bothering to turn around.

Stephanie was incredulous, disbelieving. She could see the expression on his face and she noted that he looked weary and defeated. "Jonas, why are you really here?" she asked in a soft whisper.

He smiled then, a sad smile that didn't reach his eyes. "I'm afraid I have a mutiny on my hands."

"A what?"

"Five of my top female employees are threatening to walk off their jobs."

"Five?"

"Perhaps more."

"I... I don't understand."

"For that matter, I'm having a problem comprehending it myself." He wiped a hand over his face. "This afternoon Bertha Westheimer, and four others I barely know, walked into my office."

"Bertha Westheimer?" Every bad thought she'd ever entertained about Jonas's secretary vanished in a flood of surprise and pleasure.

"Ms. Westheimer was in on this from the beginning?" His gaze captured Stephanie's, but quickly released it.

"No... just Jan, Barbara, Toni and Maureen."

His mouth formed a half-smile. "They accused me of not being hero material."

"They didn't mean anything by it—they're still upset."

"I take it that being rejected as a hero makes me the lowest of the low?" He cocked his thick brows questioningly.

"Something like that." Despite the seriousness of the conversation, Stephanie was forced to disguise a smile. "This whole thing started because Jan and the others thought I was heroine material—they were mistaken about me as well. I did everything wrong."

"How's that?" He turned and leaned against the windowsill, studying her.

She shrugged, lowered her gaze and rubbed the palms of her hands together nervously. "You kissed me once in your office, and I told you never to let it happen again. I was forever saying and doing the worst possible thing."

"But I did kiss you again."

This was a subject Stephanie wanted to avoid. "What else did they say?"

"Just that if I let you go I would be making the biggest mistake of my life, and that they refused to stand idly by and let it happen."

"What did they suggest you do now?"

"They said if I didn't do something to prevent you from leaving they were handing in their resignations effective that minute."

Looking at him was impossible; it hurt far too much. "So that's why you offered me my old job back—you were seeking a compromise?"

"No," he said harshly. "I figured if you agreed to that, then there'd be hope of you agreeing to more."

"More?"

"The ring's in my pocket, Stephanie." He brought it out and handed it to her. "It's yours."

The diamond felt warm in her palm, as though he'd repeatedly run his fingers over it. She raised her eyes to his, not understanding. "Jonas," she whispered through the tight knot that formed in her throat. "I can't accept this ring."

He went pale. "Why not?"

"For the same reason I refuse to go back to Lockwood Industries."

"I love you, Stephanie."

"But not enough to want me as your wife," she said accusingly, feeling more wretched than the day he'd fired her. "Don't worry about Jan and the others; I'll explain everything. You needn't worry about them quitting. That's the reason you're here, isn't it?"

"No," he said huskily; he paused, and seemed to regain control of his emotions. "I don't want you to leave. I thought about what you said, and you're right. If you go, everything I've ever dreamed about will disappear with you. I have my pride, Stephanie, but it's been cold comfort the last few days."

"Oh, Jonas, don't tease me, I don't think I could bear it—are you saying you want me for your wife?"

"Lord, yes." He raised his eyes toward heaven as if to plead for patience. "What did you think I was asking?"

"I don't know."

He reached for her, drawing her soft body to his and inhaling the fresh sunshine scent of her hair. "I've been half out of my mind the last few days. To be honest, I was glad Ms. Westheimer and the others came. It gave me the excuse I needed to contact you. Right after you left it dawned on me that I'd been an idiot. I'd overreacted to that stupid marriage pool. Why should any of that silliness matter to me when I've got you?" He pressed his mouth hungrily down on hers. Swiftly her lips parted, and their tongues met.

Stephanie melted against him. Tears of happiness flooded her lashes, and she sniffled loudly. "I love you so much."

"I know." His chin rubbed against the top of her head. "I think we fooled the odds makers this time."

"How's that?"

"Odds were three to one that we'd get back together again."

"Three to one?"

"You know what else?"

"No," she said with a watery smile.

"There are other odds floating around the office. They say you'll be pregnant by the end of the year."

"That soon?" She wound her arms around Jonas's neck and moved her body against his, telling him without words her eagerness to experience all that marriage had to offer them.

"I say they're way off," he growled in her ear. "It shouldn't take nearly that long."

*　*　*　*　*

An enticing
new historical romance!

Spring Will Come
SHERRY DeBORDE

It was 1852, and the steamy South was in its last hours of gentility. Camille Braxton Beaufort went searching for the one man she knew she could trust, and under his protection had her first lesson in love....

Take 4 Silhouette Special Edition novels and a surprise gift
FREE

hen preview 6 brand-new books—delivered to your door as soon as they come off the presses! you decide to keep them, you pay just $2.25 each*—an 18% saving off the retail price, *with o additional charges for postage and handling.*

Romance is alive, well and flourishing in the moving love stories of Silhouette Special Edion novels. They'll awaken your desires, enliven your senses and leave you tingling all over th excitement.

Start with 4 Silhouette Special Edition novels and a surprise gift absolutely FREE. They're urs to keep without obligation. You can always return a shipment and cancel at any time. Simply fill out and return the coupon today!

2.50 each plus 69¢ postage and handling per shipment in Canada.

Silhouette Special Edition®

Silhouette Romance

Next month some of your all-time favorites are returning to the Silhouette Romance Line. And the celebration doesn't end there—next we have the month of continuing stars. Don't miss it—come home to Romance.

"Homecoming Celebration"

COMING NEXT MONTH

ATTRACTIVE, SPACE SAVING BOOK RACK

Display your most prized novels on this handsome and sturdy book rack. The hand-rubbed walnut finish will blend into your library decor with quiet elegance, providing a practical organizer for your favorite hard-or soft-covered books.

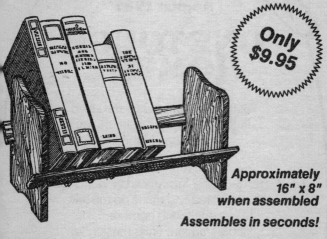

Only $9.95

**Approximately
16" x 8"
when assembled**

Assembles in seconds!

To order, rush your name, address and zip code, along with a check or money order for $10.70* ($9.95 plus 75¢ postage and handling) payable to *Silhouette Books*.

Silhouette Books
Book Rack Offer
901 Fuhrmann Blvd.
P.O. Box 1396
Buffalo, NY 14269-1396

BKR-2A

Offer not available in Canada.

*New York and Iowa residents add appropriate sales tax.

**Available
August 1987**

ONE TOUGH HOMBRE

Visit with characters introduced
in the acclaimed Desire trilogy
by Joan Hohl!

The *Hombre* is back!
J. B. Barnet—first introduced in *Texas Gold*—
has returned and make no mistake,
J.B. *is* one tough hombre...but
Nicole Vanzant finds the gentle,
tender side of the former
Texas Ranger.

Don't miss *One Tough Hombre*—
J.B. and Nicole's story.
And coming soon from Desire is
Falcon's Flight—the story of Flint Falcon
and Leslie Fairfield.

D372-1R